Financial Abuse Recovery:

Financial Healing and Empowerment After Surviving an Abusive Relationship

Authors:

Christine E. Murray, Ph.D., LCMHC/LMFT (North Carolina), LPC/LMFT (Pennsylvania)

Eileen Martin, MSW, LCSW

While every precaution has been taken in the preparation of this book, the publisher assumes no responsibility for errors or omissions, or for damages resulting from the use of the information contained herein.

FINANCIAL ABUSE RECOVERY

First edition. December 6, 2024.

ISBN: 979-8230557005

Written by Christine E. Murray and Eileen Martin.

Table of Contents

Dedication and Authors' Notes

Dedications:

Christine Murray: I dedicate this book to my sons, Evan and Bryce. You two have been my "why" for pursuing financial well-being in my personal life. Thank you for coming along for the journey.

Eileen Martin: I dedicate this book to all survivors of abuse. Your strength, resilience, and courage are a testament to the power of the human spirit. May you find healing, hope, and the knowledge that your story matters. You are more than what happened to you, and you are deserving of love, peace, and a life filled with light.

Authors' Notes:

This book is written to provide general information about the topics covered herein, specifically related to financial abuse and the process of healing and recovering from past abuse. This book is not a resource for individualized advice or services. To help connect readers with additional information and resources regarding individualized services, we created a website to accompany this book, which can be found at www.sourceforsurvivors.info/financialabuse.

Should you need additional support while reading this book, we recommend connecting with local crisis resources or a trained victim advocate or mental health professional in your community. The book's website (sourceforsurvivors.info/financialabuse) includes information about these kinds of resources. In the United States, two examples of relevant crisis resources include the National Domestic Violence

Hotline (www.thehotline.org) and the 9-8-8 Lifeline for mental health crises (https://988lifeline.org/).

Finally, please note that, unless otherwise noted, all case examples and scenarios are hypothetical and are not based on any individual person or relationship.

Chapter 1
Introduction

Natalie got an email from her bank alerting her that someone tried to open new credit cards using her name, Social Security Number, and other private information. She first suspected random identity theft, but after she and the bank investigated the matter further, they discovered that her recent ex-boyfriend was the one who attempted to open the accounts. Unfortunately, Natalie was not too surprised about this because of the reasons she had ended the relationship. After all, he was angry, abusive, and immature. However, she felt violated when she learned the extent to which he would go to hurt and take advantage of her, even after their relationship ended. She was left wondering whether she should pursue criminal charges or simply work with the bank to address the issue, and she feared retribution from her ex if she reached out to law enforcement about the identity theft.

Pamela and her husband of nearly 15 years have two elementary school-age children. Pamela has decided she wants to leave her marriage after years of physical, emotional, and verbal abuse by her husband. However, she hasn't yet told her husband about this decision because she knows she must carefully plan her exit for her and her children's safety. Pamela has been a stay-at-home mom since their first child was born nine years ago. She loves being at home with her children, although she realizes she would not likely be able to continue with that arrangement if she ended her marriage. Even though Pamela and her family live in a high-end neighborhood, drive nice cars, and take regular vacations, she has zero access to any of the family's financial resources. Her husband has always controlled the finances and doesn't allow Pamela access to the couple's money. Therefore, she's afraid and uncertain whether and how to leave her husband.

Jason and his partner ended their relationship about three months ago, but Jason's mental health continues to be impacted by the trauma of the abuse he faced in that relationship. His partner was mainly emotionally abusive, but he was also physically abusive at times. It had been Jason's first significant romantic relationship with a man since he came out as gay to a few close friends over a year ago. He hasn't told his family or work colleagues about his sexual orientation, primarily because he's heard his boss make homophobic remarks. Jason's ex used to threaten to "out" him at work and with his family if he left the relationship. Although that hasn't happened yet, Jason is afraid his ex may retaliate at some point. Because of his stress, Jason's work performance has declined, so he's worried he may lose his job. The cost of therapy also adds financial stress into the mix, but Jason is committed to going to therapy because he knows that the support his therapist is providing is helping right now.

If you're a survivor of an abusive relationship, some of the experiences in the stories of Natalie, Pamela, or Jason may resonate with you. These scenarios—all hypothetical—illustrate just a few of the many possible ways that abusive relationships can significantly and negatively affect survivors' financial well-being.

The financial effects of abuse are layered on top of many other potential impacts of abusive relationships, including impacts on survivors' physical, mental, and emotional health, relationships with others (including their children if they are parents), and educational and career pathways. Financial stress can complicate the already long, challenging process of healing and recovering from past abuse. Financial challenges are common for many survivors, so you are not alone if you're facing financial consequences in the aftermath of an abusive relationship you experienced.

Abuse is about power and control. Abusers can be relentless with all the tactics they use to gain and maintain this power and control over their partners. When people think of the term *domestic violence*, the image that often comes to mind is physical violence, and far too many people do, indeed, experience physical violence at the hands of a partner who should be there to love and care for them. However, intimate partner violence is not limited only to physical violence, and abusers often use many other tactics to gain or maintain power and control over their partners. These include emotional, verbal, and psychological abuse, as well as social isolation, sexual abuse, and financial abuse. Chapter 3 of this book contains an in-depth discussion of financial abuse, which refers to when abusers target their partners' financial well-being as a power and control tactic. Examples of financial abuse include limiting access to financial resources or information, committing fraud, and interfering with a victim's economic independence through their career or educational pathways.

Whether or not you've experienced direct financial abuse, as a survivor, you may have faced financial repercussions during and after the abusive relationship. Our aim in this book is to offer encouragement, practical guidance, and information to support survivors of past abuse as they recover from the financial impacts of abusive relationships. We believe financial well-being is an integral part of the abuse recovery process because our finances are closely intertwined with other aspects of our well-being, including our health, relationships, and educational and career goals. Below is a list with just a few examples of how improved financial well-being can support survivors' healing in these areas.

Examples of the Benefits of Greater Financial Well-Being in Different Areas of Life

Physical Health:

- Increased access to healthcare providers
- Reduced physical effects of toxic stress due to ongoing financial stressors
- Access to resources that promote physical health and well-being, such as nutritious food or a fitness center membership

Mental and Emotional Health:

- More access to mental health services, such as individual or group therapy
- Reduced emotional distress due to ongoing financial stressors
- The confidence that comes from setting and reaching financial goals (e.g., paying down debt or reaching a savings milestone)

Family and Friend Relationships:

- For parents/caregivers: Access to services and supportive resources for their children
- The ability to afford to travel to visit supportive friends and family members who live at a distance
- The ability to afford leisure activities to enhance time spent with friends and family members

Education and Career Goals:

- The ability to pay for more education or job skills training
- The ability to afford child/dependent care during work time
- Financial stability during times of job transitions (e.g., leaving or losing a job; starting a new business)

In the rest of this first chapter, we'll explore why this book is needed, how we define *financial abuse recovery,* and why we're so passionate about this important topic. We'll also provide suggestions on how to use the information in this book.

Why This Book is Needed

Awareness about domestic violence in general, and financial abuse in particular, has grown a lot over the past few decades. Of course, much more work still needs to be done to continue to educate communities about abusive relationships, as well as to increase the availability of services and resources for victims and survivors. Financial abuse remains one of the lesser-known forms of abuse, although attention has grown in recent years. For example, the well-known insurance company Allstate has made financial abuse a focus of their work through their philanthropic Allstate Foundation (n.d.).

Even with increased public awareness of the dynamics of domestic violence and financial abuse, more information and resources are still very much needed to support survivors along the long-term process of healing from past abuse, including aspects of recovery related directly and indirectly to financial well-being.

We'll talk more about our personal and professional experiences related to abuse recovery in the next section. For now, we'll share that we (Christine and Eileen) are both survivors who also have focused much of our careers on understanding and supporting abuse survivors. On a personal note, we've each seen firsthand how abuse impacted our financial well-being, as well as how complex the overall healing process can be. Through our professional careers, we've both also met many survivors whose healing journeys were made more difficult because of the financial effects of abuse.

We've written this book for anyone facing the financial repercussions of an abusive intimate relationship. This includes survivors who faced direct financial abuse, as well as those who experienced more general financial impacts of any other forms of abuse. If an abusive relationship has impacted your financial well-being, we hope this book will offer you hope that recovery (both financial and in general) is possible, along with practical tools and guidance to put that hope into action.

One reason we're so "invested in" (pun intended) this topic is that we've both seen—personally and in our work—how improved financial well-being offers survivors tangible support and confidence that help with healing processes in other areas, too. Financial healing is often a much more concrete aspect of the healing journey than other parts. Practically speaking, we can track our progress toward financial goals, such as watching our debt go down or the balance of our savings account increase. These are actual numbers (e.g., reducing debt from $1,000 to $950), which is way more concrete progress than we often see in other healing areas.

If only it were so easy to track other aspects of our healing progress, such as how much more confidence we've gained or how much less we react to triggers that remind us of our past abuse! The tangible aspects of financial well-being make it a powerful window into survivors' overall healing processes. We believe that when survivors make specific financial recovery gains, this can translate into greater overall confidence. As a bonus, a more stable financial picture also increases survivors' access to other resources (e.g., counseling, education) that cost money to tap into even more support for their healing.

Healing from past abuse is possible, even for survivors with little to no financial resources. If you have extremely limited financial resources right now, be sure to check out the special notes about this topic later in this chapter. There are many low- to no-cost steps toward healing that survivors can take, and there are often free or low-cost resources available through local community agencies (e.g., support groups offered by domestic violence service providers; books available through public libraries) and online (e.g., through credible organizations that provide educational resources). We've included a list of resources like these on the website for this book, which you can find at www.sourceforsurvivors.info/financialabuse.

Many survivors of past abuse face a reality that financial stress and limited financial resources are making their recovery process more challenging. The common saying, "Money can't buy happiness," is partially true because many ingredients for happiness—like healthy relationships or a sense of inner peace—are priceless. However, ignoring the realities of financial stress doesn't make them go away. For survivors of past abuse, financial resources are essential to the healing process for at least two main reasons:

First, more financial resources help survivors have more access to services, individualized professional guidance, and other tangible resources to support their progress and healing. Examples of resources that may be more accessible for survivors with more financial resources include legal services (especially if they are embroiled in costly court cases involving their abusers) and mental and physical healthcare, as well as the ability to secure housing, transportation, childcare, and food.

Second, reducing financial stressors can remove a significant source of emotional distress that impacts survivors' overall well-being in many areas of life. Financial stress often spills over into our relationships and mental health. Gaining a more stable financial foundation can help survivors feel more at ease, especially if financial stressors are taking a toll.

Access to more money often means access to more choices—choices to pursue new opportunities, seek out personalized professional support, and pursue goals that involve financial costs, such as starting a new small business or pursuing higher education. More access to financial resources can unlock new levels of support and enhance the healing process. Financial empowerment, therefore, is an essential part of the overall healing process for many survivors of past abuse.

Defining Financial Abuse Recovery

In this book, the term *financial abuse recovery* has a dual meaning, depending on how we bracket off the words within the term:

The first meaning is [financial abuse] recovery, referring to the process of recovering from direct experiences of financial abuse. With this meaning, we're addressing survivors whose abusers used financial-focused abuse tactics to exert power and control over them during and after the relationship. We'll talk about financial abuse in depth in Chapter 3.

The second meaning is financial [abuse recovery], and here we're referring to the economic aspects of the overall abuse recovery process. With this meaning, we're focusing on the financial components of the overall healing process from a past abusive relationship, whether or not that relationship directly involved financial abuse as a specific form of abuse perpetrated by the abuser.

Survivors who experienced direct financial abuse often face unique challenges in their healing process. These challenges can vary based on the exact nature and dynamics of the financial abuse they experienced. However, whether or not direct financial abuse was a part of your own experiences of abuse, you're likely facing at least some financial consequences of that abuse since you picked up a copy of this book.

Regardless of whether or not you faced financial abuse in your abusive relationship, you can recover, heal, and achieve well-being in your finances and your life overall. The Consumer Financial Protection Bureau (n.d.), an agency of the U.S. government, defines financial well-being as "a condition wherein a person can fully meet current and ongoing financial obligations, can feel secure in their financial future, and is able to make choices that allow them to enjoy life" (paragraph 2).

Re-read this definition of financial well-being, and take a moment to reflect on the following questions as you think about your current progress toward achieving financial well-being:

- To what extent are you currently able to meet your financial needs?

- To what extent do you feel confident and secure about your financial future?

- Do you have adequate financial resources right now to feel like you can make your own choices and enjoy your life?

It's possible you've read this definition, reflected on the questions above, and are feeling overwhelmed or hopeless about your current financial situation, in whole or in part due to the repercussions of the abuse you experienced. If that's the case, know that these feelings are a natural and expected reaction to facing barriers to experiencing financial well-being. Be gentle with these and any other feelings that come up for you along your healing journey and as you read this book.

However, know that you can have these feelings *and* learn to trust your ability to move toward financial well-being and overall healing. The pathway to get there may not be easy, but you are worthy of healing, wholeness, and a positive future in your finances and all other areas of your life. In fact, we believe that an intentional healing journey can lead you to become stronger and in an even better position—financially and in life overall—than you were before the abuse and perhaps even more than you've ever imagined possible for yourself. We call this *healing richer*.

Healing richer doesn't necessarily mean you'll automatically become financially rich in the sense of having a million dollars in the bank or being able to retire early (although, of course, these definitions of being "rich" may be possible for you, and we invite you to dream big!). What we mean by healing richer is that you can envision for yourself what a rich, full life would look like. Then, you can take steps to one day experience greater freedom on the other side of the oppressive, controlling, abusive relationship you were in. It is possible that survivors may not only be "made whole" in the sense of being restored to the version of themselves that they were before the abusive relationship began. In addition, they actually can become stronger, more empowered and fulfilled, and even more financially secure than they could ever have imagined before or during the abusive relationship.

We're confident in painting a vision for *healing richer* because we've both seen this play out in our own lives, as we'll describe in the next section.

Why This Book Is Important to Us

We're writing this book together as long-time friends and colleagues who have also supported each other through different aspects of our personal healing journeys. We first met about ten years ago through community-based advocacy efforts focusing on raising awareness about domestic violence. Our friendship and work collaborations have grown since then, and we've come to appreciate how our individual experiences share a lot in common, while also recognizing how unique each of our stories is.

This book is an extension of our professional work. Still, it's also meaningful on a personal level because of our own experiences with the financial aspects of recovering from past abusive relationships in our own lives. So, we want to take a few moments to introduce ourselves to set the stage for the rest of the book. For the rest of this book, we'll generally be writing in our collaborative voice (i.e., using "we/us" to share our collaborative thinking on this subject), but below, you'll have a chance to hear from each of us individually.

Christine's "Why"

I've been on my journey of healing from a past abusive relationship for many years now. My past abusive relationship significantly impacted my finances in a lot of ways, including the costs of legal and mental health services, as well as other direct costs related to ending the relationship. I also faced some blows to my self-confidence around finances due to the gaslighting and manipulation that my abuser used as part of money-related psychological abuse.

I'd already been in the healing process for several years when I started to develop an interest in learning about personal finances. I don't recall ever learning much about personal finance during my K-12 or college education, and it is still common for many high schoolers to graduate without a course on the subject. [For interesting statistics on this topic, check out the live U.S. Dashboard operated by the nonprofit Next Gen Personal Finance (n.d.), which shows the number of states requiring high school students to take personal finance courses. As of fall 2024, the number was 26 states, representing exciting growth from just eight states in 2020.]

Because I didn't learn much about financial literacy growing up, to some extent, I was initially "winging it" when it came to managing money during my early adult years. However, I was hooked when I started learning about personal finances through the first books I read on the topic! My interest in personal finance grew into a huge passion, and I dove in deep. I read all the financial books and magazines I could get my hands on, and then I graduated to listening to lots and lots of personal finance podcasts as well.

For several years now, I've considered learning about personal finance to be a bit of a hobby of mine. In addition to the information I've absorbed by reading and listening to financial experts, I've also learned much through trial and error in my finances. The more I learned about personal finances, the more I began to see connections to the topics of abuse recovery and domestic violence, which have long been the focus of my professional work. These connections became very personal as well because I also started to see more and more how my personal finance journey has been a significant part of my abuse recovery process.

Since my past abusive relationship ended, I experienced a few major financial messes to clean up. I approached these situations by setting financial goals, mapping out action plans, and tracking my progress. I've used similar processes to go beyond cleaning up financial messes to striving to move toward my own personal vision for financial well-being in my life. I learned that many practical strategies and actions that can be used to help clean up financial messes also apply to other financial goals, such as starting to invest and saving for big goals, like supporting my two teenage sons in their potential future college studies.

I've had the idea for this book in my heart for several years. I knew at some point I'd be ready to bring together my passion for personal finances and my mission for my work to support survivors of past abuse through this book, and the time has come! I'm thrilled that Eileen wanted to join me in creating this book as a resource for fellow survivors. As you'll read below, she has unique experiences and perspectives that add to the richness of the information we'll cover throughout this book.

Eileen's "Why"

When Christine shared her vision for this book, I was immediately drawn to her passion for supporting survivors in achieving financial wellness. While there are many books and resources focused on healing from abuse, few address the specific challenge of rebuilding financial stability after abuse. If we want to truly help survivors safely leave abusive relationships, we must ensure they feel secure and capable and have the resources needed to build a strong foundation for their future. Personally, financial abuse played a major role in keeping me feeling trapped in my past abusive relationship. I also grew up in a household where finances were only discussed when problems arose, making money a source of fear and stress. That financial anxiety was a major barrier to the freedom I eventually found.

When I first gained my freedom, I had very little knowledge of how to create a realistic budget and lacked confidence in my ability to manage my finances. I wasn't sure how I would make it on my own, and I struggled to find helpful resources. Fear once again was in the driver's seat. It took time, and a few setbacks, for me to slowly emerge from financial hardship and start feeling more confident in my ability to make sound decisions.

My hope for this book is that it offers readers practical tools to move forward in pursuing their goals, along with the support and validation needed to navigate the challenges ahead. As you read, I hope you remember who you are beyond the narrative of abuse. We can reclaim our right to live in a safe, affirming environment, one step at a time.

Our Shared "Why"

Together, we also share several reasons for wanting to write this book, which are reflected in the following three big-picture takeaway messages you'll see woven throughout the book:

First, there are many potentially significant financial consequences of abusive relationships, and yet many survivors lack information and resources to help them address the financial aspects of their healing journeys. We hope this book will be a resource to help fill this gap. With each survivor who gains greater economic independence and financial well-being, the world gains another person with the knowledge and skills to build a solid financial foundation for their lives, families, and communities.

Second, personal finance can be an intimidating topic. However, it is possible to increase your financial literacy and reduce your fears or anxieties about managing your finances. If you feel like you're starting from scratch, you can begin by learning basic, introductory information and build on that over time. On the other hand, some readers may feel like you've already got some financial know-how. In that case, you can continue to grow in this area as you work toward overcoming the economic repercussions of abuse and increase your sense of financial well-being and security. From whatever point you're starting, your finances can be an area of life in which you gain greater confidence and belief in yourself as you set and work toward goals and increase your financial freedom and empowerment.

Third, focusing on financial well-being offers survivors powerful opportunities for healing and growth. Tracking your progress toward your financial goals is often concrete, and even small steps forward can lead to big long-term gains and significant forward-moving progress. By building your financial knowledge, skills, and resources, you can create more choices and opportunities in other areas of life. More choices and opportunities can help you feel more empowered and free, which are truly priceless feelings for survivors of abuse.

A Special Message for Survivors Facing Extreme Financial Hardship

As we set out to write this book, we were deeply mindful of the severe financial distress that some survivors face in the aftermath of an abusive relationship. Financial distress may also be layered on top of other types of distress, including mental health challenges, legal or custody issues, and physical health repercussions from the abusive relationship. Our goal is to foster hope for healing and recovery, but we also recognize the gravity of the challenges you may be confronting.

This section is dedicated to any readers who are currently facing extreme financial hardship. We invite you to hold on to hope for a brighter future, even in the most challenging circumstances. Remember, even if your financial recovery process takes a very long time, you can still take steps forward—no matter how small they may feel—toward creating more stability and prosperity in your finances and your life overall.

For many survivors, the path to financial recovery can feel insurmountable. This is especially likely if you're starting from a place of extreme hardship. Some survivors wind up completely cut off from all financial resources, trapped in situations in which their abusers control every aspect of their finances, facing expensive court cases, or burdened with a mountain of debt. If you are currently facing extreme financial distress, the reality of your situation is likely both incredibly painful and challenging, and we acknowledge just how difficult this path can be. While there are no easy solutions, there is hope—and with careful planning, determination, and support, you can begin to rebuild your financial life.

If you're starting from scratch or even from a place of deep financial distress, know that you are not alone and that change, though often slow and difficult, is possible. You may begin by taking small yet meaningful steps to create a financial safety net for yourself. This could include secretly and safely saving money when possible, perhaps with the help of a trusted friend or relative who can hold onto some money for you. It also may help to connect with resources and support organizations in your community, such as nonprofits that offer clothing, food, and housing assistance. Be creative and intentional as you gather some of the initial resources you need right now.

When starting from scratch - or even a deficit - the financial abuse recovery journey won't be easy, and it's natural to feel overwhelmed by the gravity of your situation. However, it is important to hold onto hope, even when it seems out of reach. Remember that it's never too late to learn the basics of financial management and to begin building a solid foundation in this area. No matter your age or current circumstances, starting anew is always possible. Just as some older adults return to college in their 50s, 60s, and beyond, reclaiming your financial future is possible at *any* age, and the passage of time can be harnessed intentionally to work toward the life you desire.

As much as possible, try to hold onto that hope. We know this isn't easy. Remember that the road ahead may be challenging, but every step forward—whether big or small—can bring you closer to financial freedom and safety. Your journey may be long and winding, but you have the courage and resilience within you to build a better future, and you can also connect with supportive information and resources to help strengthen you along the way.

How to Use This Book

Please let your unique needs, life history, and financial circumstances guide your experience reading this book. Our goal was to write it in a way that's both general enough to apply to survivors facing very different life circumstances and detailed enough so each reader can apply the book's messages to their unique situation.

Of course, like all books written for a general audience, we offer a disclaimer that this book is not intended to be individualized advice or guidance tailored to your situation. For that level of personalized services, we included a list of resource directories on the book's website (www.sourceforsurvivors.info/financialabuse) to help you connect with trained professionals who can offer individualized support and services. Because financial abuse recovery involves many dimensions of survivors' lives, the types of services and support each person may need will vary. These may include mental health professionals, job skill training programs, financial advising, and consumer credit counseling.

As you read this book, focus on the information that applies to you, your current life circumstances, and your future goals. We wouldn't be offended if you skip over sections that don't apply to you! If it would be helpful, consider working through this book with a trained counselor, peer support group, a trusted friend or family member, or an accountability partner. (We'll talk more about accountability partners in Chapter 7.)

Here are additional suggestions for getting the most out of this book:

First, remember that there's no need for any shame or self-judgment based on your current starting point along your healing and recovery journey, including in the area of your finances. Stigma and shame often surround both experiences of having been in an abusive relationship *and* specific money-related experiences, circumstances, and challenges.

Christine and her colleague, Allison Crowe at East Carolina University, have done a series of studies and developed a social media campaign around the topic of the stigma surrounding intimate partner violence. The See the Triumph campaign (www.seethetriumph.org)

launched in January 2013, and we've heard from many survivors through both the research and outreach related to this campaign about how they faced internal and external stigma related to their abuse.

It's also natural to have areas of shame or embarrassment around our finances. This may stem from feeling embarrassed about lacking financial knowledge or specific circumstances, such as your debt or a lack of savings. Financial shame is not unique to survivors of abuse, and indeed, shame is a common emotion that comes up for many people around their finances (Bechard, 2022). Researchers (Gladstone et al., 2021) have discussed how "financial shame spirals" make it more challenging to break free from difficult financial circumstances. Shame can become layered on top of difficult financial circumstances and make it more difficult to move toward greater financial well-being.

The stigma and shame surrounding both abusive relationships and financial challenges can be intense and intertwined for survivors. This may be especially true if your abuser said or did things to put you down for a lack of knowledge, skills, or competence in the area of your finances. For example, they may have said, "You're terrible with money, so I'll just handle everything," or ridiculed and belittled you for having debt or making past mistakes with money.

If you feel any degree of shame, embarrassment, or stigma because of the abuse you experienced or your current financial situation, remember that you are not alone. We have also felt this way at different points in our journeys. We've also seen these feelings play out for many survivors we've encountered through our work. Throughout this book, we focus on helping readers work through those feelings and move toward a greater sense of self-confidence and self-worth along their healing journey overall and in the area of their finances.

Also, know that even if you *feel* stigma or shame about your experiences with abuse or your finances, this does not mean any level of stigma or shame is warranted. First, if any shame is warranted related to the abuse that happened, it should be carried entirely by the abuser, not you as the person who was the target of their abusive words and actions. We'll talk more about this topic in Chapter 5.

Second, we would venture to guess that virtually every adult over the age of 30 (if not younger!) has made financial decisions in the past that they view as mistakes. Some of us make more significant mistakes than others, but it's unrealistic to expect perfection in our finances (not to mention any other area of life). The best we can do along the journey to financial well-being is to learn from our mistakes and keep moving toward a more positive future.

If you think about it, both of these topics—abusive relationships and finances—aren't subjects most people discuss in regular, day-to-day conversation. Chances are, you interact with people every day in person or online who have been in an abusive relationship or who are navigating challenging financial circumstances. You just might not know it because people don't typically mention these sensitive topics in casual conversations.

It's tempting to look at other people's lives and assume they have it all figured out. Remember that you have no idea what most other people have been through in life, and try to stay focused on taking the next steps toward *your* goals. Releasing shame and stigma surrounding abuse or financial challenges isn't easy, but it is possible. This book offers encouragement and practical strategies to support you along the way, especially in Chapter 5, which focuses on committing to a shame-free, empowered recovery process.

Second, take good care of yourself while reading this book and through all other aspects of your healing journey. Self-care has become somewhat of a buzzword in recent years, but that doesn't take away from the fact that practicing self-care is an essential tool to use during the process of healing from past abuse. While the healing journey can be rewarding, it's also challenging. It's common for survivors of abuse to experience emotional triggers, distressing emotions, or painful or traumatic memories as they navigate the healing process.

Be sure to pace yourself and be sensitive to your emotional reactions while reading this book. We suggest that you have coping resources and strategies in place before diving too deeply into emotionally intense topics. Some possible coping tools that might be helpful include seeking counseling, reaching out for emotional and practical support from trusted friends or family members, going to support groups, and practicing strategies like relaxation breathing or mindfulness meditation.

Just in case any seriously distressing emotions arise, it's helpful to know about crisis response resources available to offer support on a 24/7/ 365 basis. In the United States, one helpful resource is the National Domestic Violence Hotline (https://www.thehotline.org/). Another mental health-focused crisis line is the 9-8-8 Lifeline (https://988lifeline.org). If you're a reader outside of the United States, be sure to identify the similar resources available to you.

Take good care of yourself, practice patience, and move gently and with as much ease as possible as you read through this book to get the most out of it while honoring your emotional and mental health and safety.

Third, remember that some aspects of financial well-being are within your sphere of influence, but also recognize the broader economic climate and other factors that are primarily out of your control. When it comes to our finances (as in most areas of life), having a healthy dose of optimism is helpful. Both of us (Christine and Eileen) consider ourselves to be optimists but with a dose of realism. Having a positive, optimistic outlook in life can be a beautiful thing. Still, it helps to be mindful that our rose-colored glasses don't become too rosy to the point that we overlook the reality of external circumstances that can impact our progress toward our goals and healing.

In all areas of our lives, including in our finances, there will always be some factors within our control and others over which we have no control or influence. This truth is likely very familiar to those who've faced an abusive relationship. No matter how much we may have asked our abusers to change their hurtful actions, we likely eventually realized that we couldn't make the other person do things they didn't want to take accountability for.

It's possible that even today, your abuser is continuing to try and hurt you in the area of your finances. It's also possible you're facing other external challenges that you have little to no control over—such as a boss who refuses to give you a raise even after proving time and again what an excellent employee you are, high costs for parenting-related expenses and child care, or a family member who won't pay back the money you loaned them years ago.

In recent years, thanks in large part to the impacts and aftermath of the COVID-19 pandemic, we've all had a first-hand glimpse into how volatile local, national, and global economies can be. Costs soared due to rising inflation and supply chain issues, people lost or left their jobs in light of changing workplace conditions, and many families took on more debt to cover basic living expenses. The need for survivors—and virtually everyone else—to focus on their financial well-being has perhaps never been greater in light of recent economic conditions.

It can feel overwhelming to consider all of the external, uncontrollable factors that impact our finances. Often, it helps to practice self-compassion (see Dr. Kristin Neff's website, www.self-compassion.org, for helpful resources on this topic), be intentional about processing these feelings in healthy ways, and acknowledge that they are normal and understandable. At the same time, it's helpful to find a balance between acknowledging the realities of external conditions while also staying focused on the steps that we can take within our sphere of influence and control.

Stay encouraged by focusing on positive progress and taking the next right steps for you instead of aiming for perfection and trying to reach your goals at lightning speed. Over time, you'll likely find that the more you focus on what you *do* have the power to control, the more external factors will cause less distress and turmoil in your finances and other areas of life.

Finally, on a practical note, consider what approach to reading this book will work best for you, and go for it. We wrote this book knowing that each reader's circumstances will be unique. Although we're sure most readers will probably read the book in the normal way from start to finish, we encourage you to dive into this book in whatever way is most meaningful to you.

If that means skipping or skimming sections or chapters that don't apply to you, then you can flip past those pages guilt-free! For example, if you have a high level of financial know-how already, you may find some of the basics we cover in Chapter 8 to be too introductory. Or, if you experienced a relationship that was abusive but didn't include financial abuse, Chapter 3 may not be as relevant to you.

On the other hand, for readers who want to use this book as the basis for a deep dive into financial abuse recovery, it may help to read through it twice: once for an overview of the content and then again to map out specific goals and action plans to bring the content to life in ways that are meaningful for you. As we mentioned earlier, we recommend that readers consider this book to be a resource for general (i.e., non-personalized) information, so please consider seeking professional guidance to adapt this information to your unique circumstances.

Here's a preview of what you'll find in the pages ahead. First, two chapters focus on the intersections of abusive relationships and finances. This includes a general overview of abuse and how it can impact survivors' finances in Chapter 2 and an in-depth look at financial abuse in Chapter 3.

Then, we move into covering several dimensions of financial recovery, including how financial recovery fits into the overall healing journey for survivors of abuse (Chapter 4), how to commit to a shame-free recovery process (Chapter 5), taking stock of the status of your current financial well-being (Chapter 6), financial dreaming and goal setting (Chapter 7), essential tools and skills to enhance your financial well-being (Chapter 8), and strategies for resetting your career or educational pathway (Chapter 9). The book concludes in Chapter 10, which focuses on how healing from past abuse and moving toward financial well-being can help you build a meaningful, positive future.

Thank you for trusting us to be part of your journey by picking up this book! We hope you'll gain knowledge, skills, and encouragement to support you along the way.

Chapter 2
Financial Implications of Abusive Relationships

"Simply acknowledging it happened helped me begin the healing process."

~ Domestic Violence Survivor

The above quote reflects the powerful growth that can happen when survivors' experiences are validated within the context of understanding the common dynamics of abusive relationships. This quote was shared by a survivor of an abusive relationship who participated in a research study connected to the See the Triumph campaign that Christine co-founded, as we introduced in Chapter 1. The See the Triumph campaign's focus has been on supporting survivors and ending the stigma surrounding intimate partner violence.

As a society, we are often narrow-sighted when thinking about relationship abuse. Our minds typically go to black eyes and bruises due to media depictions of domestic violence and stereotypes about abusive relationships. These kinds of limited views about abusive relationships often miss the broader scope of abuse. While physical abuse is present and life-threatening in many abusive relationships, power and control dynamics can manifest in many different ways within abusive relationships. In addition to physical abuse, abusive relationships may include emotional and psychological abuse, sexual abuse, career and educational abuse, and financial abuse, among other forms and tactics of abuse.

Abusive relationships are complex, and their consequences can be far-reaching. People often wonder why someone stays in an abusive relationship when the relationship seems to be so harmful. Fear of violence, social isolation, fear of being unworthy of love, and concerns about one's children are just some of the many powerful motivators for staying silent and not being able to leave an abusive relationship. Another common reason that survivors may stay in abusive relationships is due to financial challenges or dependence on their abusers, and this can be true for survivors across different socioeconomic statuses. Many abusers use financial control as one way to entrap their partners in an abusive relationship. In addition, financial fears are another primary reason many victims stay, regardless of their socio-economic status. When victims have limited access to economic resources, their perpetrators maintain more power and control within the relationship, and victims may not have access to any financial resources that would allow them to be able to leave the relationship and rebuild their lives.

In this chapter, we take a look at the dynamics of abusive relationships and how they often intersect with survivors' financial well-being. This chapter will set the stage for our deeper dive into the specific dynamics of financial abuse that follows in Chapter 3. Throughout this chapter, you'll find self-reflection questions to help you apply the information presented to your own experiences. These self-reflection questions are useful because reflecting on our personal experiences and understanding their impact on our lives is a valuable first step toward healing.

Defining Terminology Related to Abusive Relationships

There are several terms used to describe abuse that happens within the context of an intimate relationship. Phrases like domestic violence, intimate partner violence, and abuse are often used interchangeably to describe situations in which one partner exerts power and control over the other person in a relationship to dominate, manipulate, and hurt them. While these terms are similar, for consistency, we will primarily use the term "abusive relationship" throughout this book.

Power and coercive control dynamics are the common denominator that underlies abusive relationships, and these dynamics can show up in many different types of abusive tactics and behaviors, such as physical, emotional, psychological, sexual, or financial abuse. Just because someone isn't experiencing physical violence doesn't mean other forms of violence aren't present.

In some abusive relationships, only one form of abuse (e.g., emotional abuse) may be present. However, abusers often combine multiple layers of abusive behaviors into complex, interlocking patterns of violence and abuse. As you examine your own experiences within one or more abusive relationships, one self-reflection question that you may find helpful to ponder is: *In what ways did my abuser attempt to exert power and control over me during (or after) the relationship?* Be comprehensive as you reflect on all the ways that you experienced abusive behavior patterns by your abuser, as well as how these different forms of control and abuse may have interacted with one another. For example, your abuser's emotional and verbal abuse may have led you to feel isolated and trapped in the relationship, making you more vulnerable to staying in the relationship if physical violence happened.

Let's also consider the terminology used for individuals who perpetuate abuse and exert power and control in a relationship. You may have encountered terms like "offender," "perpetrator," or "abuser." For consistency, we will primarily use the term "abuser" throughout this book.

Similarly, the terms "victim" and "survivor" are terms that may be used to describe a person who has experienced abuse and power and control dynamics within an intimate relationship. "Victim" and "survivor" often carry distinct meanings, and we will use them in a specific way throughout this book for clarity and consistency. In general, when we use the term "victim," we are referring to someone who is currently experiencing a risk of harm, injury, threats to their safety, or other losses due to being in a current relationship with an abuser. These potential risks include physical, emotional, financial, and other potential negative forms of harm.

On the other hand, we use the term "survivor" to refer to someone who has taken steps toward safety and is moving toward overcoming that abuse. In general, when we refer to a "survivor," we are referring to someone who is no longer in the abusive intimate relationship.

Therefore, in general, when you read the term "victim" throughout this book, we are referring to experiences that happen when someone is involved in a *current* relationship with an abuser. When you read the term "survivor," we are mostly referring to someone who has been in an abusive relationship that is in the *past*. That said, we acknowledge that this terminology has many limitations. First, we believe that anyone who has experience with abuse most certainly can be described as a "survivor," and people show great strength and resilience while navigating a current abusive relationship. In addition, we know there is often a blurry line between current and past relationships. Sadly, for many survivors, abuse does not necessarily end after the relationship with their abuser ends. For example, many survivors need to stay in contact with their abusers because they share custody of their children. As such, someone could meet our definition of "survivor" while also facing ongoing risks to their safety and other forms of harm.

Overall, we acknowledge that the victim/survivor terminology does not fully capture the nuances of experiences in abusive relationships. Still, we share our definitions here to try to provide as much clarity as possible for when you see these terms throughout this book. No matter which term resonates with you at this point in your journey, this book is intended to help along your healing journey, especially focusing on regaining a sense of control and empowerment over your financial future. To that end, we also highlight the concept of "thriving." Like the concept of "healing richer" that we introduced in Chapter 1, we use the term "thriving" to describe the process of moving beyond surviving and moving entirely toward recovering, healing, and reclaiming a meaningful and fulfilling life after abuse. Thriving represents a sense of freedom and empowerment, and we invite you, as you read this book, to consider what that place looks like for you.

Reflection question: What do the terms "victim," "survivor," "thriving," and "healing richer" mean to you?

How Survivors' Backgrounds and Identities Influence Experiences with Abuse

Our intention for this book was to develop a resource that is affirming and inclusive of all individuals who have been financially impacted by an abusive relationship, regardless of their gender, affectional and sexual orientation, culture, race, religion, and other background characteristics. We know that abuse can occur in any type of interpersonal relationship and across all socioeconomic and demographic backgrounds. Also, cultural, contextual, and religious beliefs and values can influence how we perceive relationships. Therefore, we invite you to apply and adapt the information we present throughout this book in a way that reflects your unique background and experiences.

Each of us has many overlapping identities. All aspects of our identities—such as our race, culture, gender, sexuality, class, religion, and/or disability status—interact to create unique experiences, belief systems, values, and potential experiences of discrimination and privilege. Every individual has a personal, evolving blueprint for their identity that is influenced by many dimensions of their backgrounds and identities. Our identities shape our views about the world around us, as well as our views about who we are as a person.

Survivors' cultural and contextual backgrounds often influence their experiences during and after abusive relationships. For example, many survivors face cultural or religious values that reinforce gender role imbalances or look down upon divorce, even in cases of abuse. Abusers may lean into these kinds of cultural values as a way to strengthen their power and control over their victims. We saw an example of this in Jason's hypothetical case study, which was presented at the start of Chapter 1. His abuser threatened to out him about his sexual orientation as part of the other power and control dynamics in their relationship.

It's important to note that survivors' backgrounds and identities also can be powerful sources of strength and connection as well. For example, cultural or spiritual healing practices may offer comfort and solace for survivors, such as when they turn to prayer or meditation to promote their healing and inner peace. Culturally responsive community resources and services—such as the opportunity to speak with a trained professional in one's native language—are very important sources of support for many survivors.

Self-determination refers to a person's ability to make choices about their life and pursue goals free from undue external control. We celebrate each survivor's personal autonomy, freedom, and agency—and we believe this is possible for survivors from all walks of life. Each survivor can examine their important identities and cultural influences in order to align their healing journey with their values and belief systems. Often, the support of a trained, culturally competent mental health professional can help this process, along with guidance from trauma-informed leaders and mentors within survivors' cultural and community contexts who understand the dynamics of abusive relationships.

Unfortunately, the cycle of abuse can disrupt our sense of self-determination by eroding our autonomy, self-worth, and perceptions about our ability to make independent decisions. The healing journey offers many opportunities for survivors from all backgrounds to regain freedom and independence. Although our focus in this book is primarily on financial well-being and recovery, we believe self-determination is important in all areas of life. As you read this book and continue along your healing journey, remember that your journey is unique. You can be empowered to move at your own pace and take the steps toward healing that feel most meaningful to you at any given point in time, while also considering the many ways your individual experiences may have been impacted by the unique identities that shape who you are.

Reflection question: What personal background influences and identities are most meaningful for you? To what extent do you think that these identities have impacted your experiences with abuse?

Understanding the Power and Control Dynamics that Underlie Abusive Relationships

Now that we've reviewed some terminology about abusive relationships and underscored the many backgrounds and identities that can impact survivors' experiences, it's time to take a deeper dive into exploring the dynamics of abusive relationships. As we noted earlier, at the core, the dynamics of abusive relationships are defined by *power and control.*

The power and control dynamics in an abusive relationship involve the abuser using a variety of tactics—which may include violence, manipulation, and threats—to assert dominance, create fear, and maintain control over the victim or survivor. Typically, abuse within an intimate relationship is a recurring pattern of behavior, not just an isolated incident, and abuse may escalate by becoming more frequent, severe, and dangerous over time.

A common myth is that abuse stems from an anger management problem. Even if anger is present for an abuser, the driving force behind abusive relationships is an abuser's desire to control and dominate their partner. Abusers' efforts to gain and maintain power and control can take many forms, including physical violence, emotional manipulation, financial abuse, isolation, and other coercive and controlling tactics.

Some abusers show overarching signs of antisocial, aggressive patterns of interacting in the world (Holtzworth-Munroe & Stuart, 1994; Jacobson & Gottman, 2007). These abusers might have a history of criminal, violent, or otherwise disruptive behavior patterns in a variety of settings (e.g., school, workplaces, and the broader community). Abusive behaviors in relationships may not seem surprising or out of character for these kinds of abusers, as their aggressive, domineering patterns often play out in multiple areas of their lives. That said, even abusive behaviors that fit into an abuser's typical ways of existing in the world can still be quite confusing and hurtful for their victims.

On the other hand, other abusers tend to limit their abusive, violent behaviors to the context of intimate relationships (Holtzworth-Munroe & Stuart, 1994; Jacobson & Gottman, 2007). For these abusers, their patterns of abuse and control are seen primarily, if not exclusively, in the context of intimate relationships. Some of these perpetrators appear outwardly happy, friendly, and engaging as they navigate the world around them. They may hold jobs, have friends, seem well-adjusted and perhaps even charming, and may even be seen as respected leaders in their communities. However, their behavior within their intimate relationship may be disturbingly different. For these abusers, this "Dr. Jekyll and Mr. Hyde" act is a form of manipulation that can deepen their victim's confusion, perhaps even leading the victim to blame themselves for the abuse. Their victims also may have a harder time reaching out for help because people they tell about the abuse may respond by saying something like, "I could never see them acting like that! They're such a good person." However, just because the abuser's dark side is seen only in the context of the relationship does not mean that it is not real and impactful for victims and survivors.

Your own abuser's actions may reflect the more generally antisocial or Jekyll/Hyde patterns described above, or they might fall somewhere in between. In recent years, there has been a lot of public attention as well to the topic of *narcissistic abuse*, meaning abuse that is carried out by someone who demonstrates narcissistic personality characteristics, and in some cases they might even meet the diagnostic criteria for Narcissistic Personality Disorder (NPD). (Keep in mind, as with all mental health disorders, NPD can only be diagnosed by a qualified professional, such as a psychiatrist, psychologist, or licensed mental health professional.)

Overall, although abusers may share some common patterns or presentations, we believe it's most helpful to examine their patterns primarily in the context of power and control dynamics. We invite you to pause and take time to reflect on the following question: *In what ways did/does my abuser attempt to gain and maintain power and control over me?* Identifying and focusing on these patterns of power and control tactics is valuable for understanding your experiences, even if your abuser doesn't fall neatly into a category like being "antisocial" or "narcissistic." However these power and control dynamics showed up in your relationship, they likely caused you a lot of hurt, pain, and confusion. As we will remind you throughout this book, you can heal from those experiences, and you deserve to be treated with love, kindness, and respect—not aggression, manipulation, and abuse.

The Cycle of Violence

Abuse often follows a pattern of behavior that can become deeply engrained into the fabric of the abusive relationship. Abusers' controlling behavior patterns often play out over time as the abuser strives to gain and maintain power and domination in the relationship. These patterns are often called the Cycle of Abuse (for example, see Craig & Kippert, 2022). The terms used to describe the phases of the Cycle of Violence vary in different sources of information about abusive relationships. However, the most common terminology we've seen includes the Honeymoon phase, the Tension-Building phase, and the Explosion phase.

We'll review these phases below, but please keep in mind that although these are common patterns that occur in abusive relationships, every person's experience is unique. If your own experiences with an abusive relationship don't completely match the description below, know that your experiences are still valid. At the same time, both of us have seen through our professional work with countless survivors just how much some version of the Cycle of Violence is a common experience for many victims and survivors. In fact, we've often seen survivors' eyes light up in a moment of self-validation when they hear about this common Cycle of Violence and realize that their own experiences are similar to these patterns.

As an aside, Christine has even remarked in many trainings and courses she has taught on the topic of domestic violence how these patterns seem so common that it is almost like abusers have taken a class somewhere to learn the strategies of being abusive toward their partners! While we don't think a "class" like this actually exists, we can speculate that harmful relational patterns are likely learned through intergenerational family patterns, gender socialization within patriarchal systems, dysfunctional relationship examples in the media, and other harmful societal messages. This could be the topic of a whole other book, so for now, let's turn our attention back to the phases of the Cycle of Violence to explore how these common patterns often play out.

During the Honeymoon phase, an abuser often woos their victim, such as through romantic gestures, flattering words, and expressions of interest and affection. In the earliest stages of the relationship, these gestures can serve the purpose of establishing an attachment between the partners. Recently, you may have heard the term *love bombing* to describe one way that the Honeymoon phase might show up in relationships.

Eventually, the glow of the Honeymoon phase begins to fade, and the Tension-Building phase begins. Here, the abuser often becomes more irritable, jealous, withdrawing, and/or controlling toward their partner. As this tension grows, it can escalate to the Explosion phase, in which the abuser uses more extreme and potentially violent and aggressive behaviors to gain or regain a sense of control over their victim. Early in the relationship, the "explosion" may not be extremely severe, but it can be hurtful nonetheless while also setting the stage for more severe violence that may emerge later.

Following the Explosion phase, the Honeymoon phase often begins again. The Cycle of Violence continues when the abuser acts apologetically for their explosive behaviors, perhaps attempting to show remorse by buying flowers, saying affectionate words, or making false promises that they won't act in hurtful ways again. However, because the abuser is deeply unwilling to accept responsibility and move toward lasting change, the tension builds again, and the cycle repeats itself, often over and over and over again.

These patterns of behavior typically are repeated time and again in abusive relationships, often desensitizing victims to the abuse. Abusers' actions during the Cycle of Violence provide intermittent rewards and punishment, which can lead to what's often called a *trauma bond*. The repetitive cycle hinges on a power imbalance in favor of the abuser, and the reward periods of calm and reconciliation often involve affection and comfort that remind the victim of the beginning of the relationship when abuse likely was not yet present.

> *Reflection question: To what extent was the experience of intermittent rewards and punishments a factor that influenced your decisions about whether to stay in your abusive relationship?*

As abusive relationships progress, abusers often test the waters to gauge victims' reactions, which can lead to further escalations of tension and violence. Over time, as the Cycle of Violence continues and the abuse becomes deeply rooted in relationships, abusers may altogether withhold any of the prior affectionate behaviors used in the Honeymoon phase. In these cases, the abuse is usually firmly entrenched within the relationship, and the abuser's power and control have been firmly established.

For victims of abuse, experiencing the Cycle of Violence can feel confusing, exhausting, and like an emotional roller coaster. They may hold out hope and focus on the good sides they have seen in their abusers, while also feeling hurt and worn down by the violence, abuse, and psychological manipulation. Even when bad times arise, they may still be holding over feelings of love and affection that grew stronger during the good times. Abusive relationships are not typically all bad, 100% of the time, and the good or calmer times may even last for a relatively longer period of time than many people realize.

We've both lived through versions of the Cycle of Violence in our own past abusive relationships, as well as we have seen it play out with many victims and survivors with whom we've worked. Learning about this Cycle can help validate survivors' feelings of confusion and self-blame. It's natural to look back on the relationship and wonder why we didn't recognize the abuse earlier on. However, learning about how abusers commonly use affection and other Honeymoon phase-type behaviors to build a sense of attachment and love can help survivors feel more compassionate and understanding about their earlier decisions within the relationship. Recognizing the extent to which your decisions and experiences were influenced by your abuser's subversive manipulative, controlling patterns can be a powerful step in your healing process.

The Financial Implications of Different Forms of Abuse

As is evident from our discussion above, the Cycle of Violence can be disorienting for victims and survivors. One important point we want to emphasize about this Cycle is that virtually any form of abuse can become part of this cycle—including physical, sexual, emotional, psychological, verbal, and financial abuse. We will discuss financial abuse in detail in Chapter 3, but in this section, we will explore the other forms of abuse, with a focus on how these different forms of abuse can have implications for victims' and survivors' financial well-being.

The information in this section about the potential financial costs of various forms of abuse is grounded in a research study that Christine and her colleagues (King et al., 2017) conducted with 130 survivors of past abusive relationships. In addition to sharing ways that their experiences with abuse impacted their financial well-being, the participating survivors estimated the total costs for out-of-pocket healthcare services related to their physical, mental, and cognitive health. There was wide variation in how many healthcare costs the survivors faced. For example, the range of estimated costs for physical healthcare costs alone was from $0 to $200,000. Of course, many survivors reported no costs, as well as some survivors who were outliers in terms of reporting very high costs. The median (i.e., the exact midpoint of reported costs between the highest and lowest amounts) estimates provide a useful statistic to examine the costs reported in each category of out-of-pocket healthcare expenses. Among participants in this sample, the median reported physical health care costs was $3,000, the median reported mental health care costs also was $3,000, and the median reported cognitive healthcare costs (e.g., for rehabilitation for a traumatic brain injury) was $1,600. As these figures show, survivors may face thousands of dollars in financial costs for healthcare expenses alone, and this does not even factor in many other potential costs, such as lost income from time missed at work.

As we stated earlier, it is often the case that abusers use many different forms of abuse at once. Below, we separately cover the topics of physical abuse, sexual abuse, and emotional, psychological, and verbal abuse. However, please keep in mind that these forms of abuse often co-occur, often alongside financial abuse as well.

Physical Abuse

According to the Domestic Violence Hotline (n.d.), "Physical abuse is one of the most easily identified types of abuse. It involves using physical violence, or threats of it, to maintain power over an individual" (paragraph 3). Abusers may use many different types of physically violent behaviors, ranging from relatively minor, non-injury-producing acts to life-threatening acts of violence. Often, the severity of physical abuse becomes more significant over time during the relationship. On the other hand, sometimes a physically violent act can occur just once or a small number of times, but even isolated incidents can be used to create fear and a sense of pending harm among victims. Keep in mind that a relationship can be abusive even if physical violence is not present. However, when physical violence *is* present in an intimate relationship, it is typically accompanied by broader power and control dynamics, such as with co-occurring psychological or emotional abuse.

Experiencing physical violence can have significant financial consequences for victims and survivors of abusive relationships. The financial costs related to physical abuse may include the following:

- Costs of medical care for injuries and chronic stress-related illness.

- Fees for medications and other treatments, such as physical or occupational therapies.

- Lost income due to abuse-related injuries and other physical ailments that lead to absenteeism from work or short- or long-term disabilities.

Physical violence can be highly distressing for victims and survivors, and we cannot understate the safety risks that may exist when there is a threat of physical violence. For this reason, we recommend that any readers facing ongoing threats of physical violence and other forms of abuse reach out to a trained professional in your community to develop a safety plan. Contact the National Domestic Violence Hotline (www.thehotline.org; 1-800-799-7233) or visit the Get Help section of their website to search for local community agencies across the United States: https://www.thehotline.org/get-help/domestic-violence-local-resources/. Safety planning is valuable in the context of any form of abuse, but it is essential and time-sensitive when there is a risk of physical violence because these situations can be very dangerous and carry significant risks for victims and survivors.

Sexual Abuse

Sexual abuse describes any form of forced or coerced sexual activity perpetrated by an abuser within an abusive relationship (Murray & Graves, 2012). At times, sexual and financial abuse may be interconnected within the broader context of power and control dynamics in abusive relationships. For example, a perpetrator might coerce, threaten, or force sexual activity if a victim requests financial support for themselves or their children.

Victims who are financially dependent on their abusers may feel compelled to comply with unwanted sexual advances and behaviors out of fear of losing financial support, shelter, or other necessities. Perpetrators also may use both sexual and economic manipulation and threats to control their victims. This might include making threats to disclose private information, ruining the victim's reputation, and harming their financial stability.

In addition to the potential interconnections between sexual and financial abuse, sexual abuse also can lead to other economic consequences for victims and survivors, such as medical costs to treat sexually transmitted infections (STIs) and the costs of mental health counseling to support healing from sexual trauma.

> *Reflection question: If you experienced any physical or sexual abuse within your abusive relationship(s), what, if any, financial consequences did you face as a result?*

Emotional, Psychological, and Verbal Abuse

Emotional, psychological, and verbal abuse are often interrelated, and sometimes, these terms are used interchangeably. We view each of these forms of abuse as being slightly different from one another based on the mechanism of power and control the abuser uses when they carry out each one (Murray & Graves, 2012). With emotional abuse, an abuser plays on a victim's *feelings and emotions* to establish power and control. Psychological abuse focuses more on *mental manipulation* and *mind control*, and verbal abuse describes an abuser's use of *hurtful, disparaging words* to diminish their victim.

Because these forms of abuse often co-occur and are layered on top of each other, we will consider their financial implications together in this section. Abusers may use many specific emotional, psychological, and verbal abuse tactics to inflict harm. Examples include disparaging words, isolation, and gaslighting. Let's look at how each of these abuse tactics can have financial implications for victims and survivors.

Disparaging words. Abusers may use criticism, insults, and other demeaning words to undermine victims' sense of self-esteem and self-worth. These hurtful words typically belittle victims' abilities, appearance, or intelligence and chip away at victims' confidence, which can further establish abusers' dominance and control. Abusers' constant stream of verbal harm often leads victims to question their value and abilities, often fostering a sense of helplessness and financial dependence on the abuser. When survivors are left feeling self-doubt and shame as a result of verbal abuse, it's natural that they start to feel less financially competent and empowered. It's understandable when victims and survivors lack self-confidence in the face of ongoing verbal abuse. Relatedly, lowered self-confidence can impact how victims and survivors show up and perform at work and affect their willingness to take risks that might lead to more significant financial opportunities (e.g., applying for higher-paying jobs or asking for promotions and raises at work).

Isolation. Abusers frequently use isolation as a tactic to control their victims by cutting them off from friends, family, and other support networks. In turn, isolation increases victims' dependency on their abusers for emotional and financial support. Often, abusers manipulate victims into believing they are the only one who truly cares about them, intensifying this dependency and making it even more challenging for victims to seek help or escape the abusive relationship. Sometimes, abusers extend their isolation tactics to victims' workplaces, such as by not allowing them to work outside the home or blocking them from forming friendships with work colleagues.

Gaslighting. Gaslighting is a psychological manipulation technique used by abusers to make victims question their perceptions, memories, or sanity. An example of gaslighting involves abusers denying their actions, causing victims to question their reality, especially if they have seen evidence of the abusers' actions (e.g., seeing a transaction in an online joint checking account that the abuser denies making).

When gaslighting behaviors continue, victims may grow to doubt their intelligence and perceptions. This manipulative tactic deepens the victim's self-doubt and further increases their reliance on the abuser. Victims and survivors who face ongoing gaslighting by their abusers run the risk of becoming less trusting in their own abilities and thinking, which could lead them to doubt their ability to manage their finances effectively over time. We'll revisit the topic of gaslighting in the context of financial abuse coming up in Chapter 3.

Overall, emotional, psychological, and verbal abuse can profoundly affect a person's self-esteem and confidence, impacting various areas of their life, including how they manage their money. Low self-esteem can make victims and survivors feel unworthy or incapable, which may translate into a lack of confidence in making financial decisions or managing money effectively. Survivors may become paralyzed by a fear of failure, which can lead them to feel hesitant to take even the slightest risks or make decisions that could improve their financial circumstances. Victims and survivors who have experienced emotional abuse might also develop a dependency on others for validation and decision-making, relying on their abusers to manage finances because they feel incapable of doing it themselves.

Reflection question: What, if any, fears led you to feel stuck in the relationship or financially dependent on your abuser?

Potential Long-Term Costs of Abuse for Victims and Survivors

Experiencing an abusive relationship can have many immediate impacts on victims and survivors. In this section, we also briefly consider the potential longer-term costs of abuse that victims and survivors may encounter regarding their finances. Overall, abuse can have significant and long-lasting effects on a person's career and educational goals, limiting survivors' financial freedom. Mental health issues—such as anxiety, depression, post-traumatic stress disorder (PTSD), and low self-esteem—may arise during or after an abusive relationship. Our environment has a significant impact on our mental health. If our environment feels unsafe due to current or historical abuse, it can get in the way of our ability to focus on our education, career, or financial goals.

Due to the pervasiveness of the power and control dynamics, victims and survivors often find it difficult to trust others. This can impact relationships with peers, teachers, colleagues, and supervisors. The lack of trust can also extend to family members and friends, meaning it can feel challenging to ask for help financially and other forms of support.

Similarly, we must consider the financial aftermath of leaving an abusive relationship. Victims often face unexpected expenses such as legal fees, loss of income from taking days off for court appearances, child care costs, and the transition to a single income. These expenses can take a toll on victims' and survivors' finances and may take a long time to overcome. For many survivors, the journey toward recovering from past abuse—including financial recovery—can be a long and complicated one.

Reflection question: What have been the most significant ways your experiences in an abusive relationship impacted your views about money and financial independence?

Conclusion

All forms of abuse can have significant short- and long-term financial repercussions for victims and survivors. This might include substantial costs for treatments to address physical injuries and conditions resulting from the abuse, as well as the costs of counseling or therapy to support the healing journey from the mental health implications of trauma and abuse. Experiencing abuse can impact victims' and survivors' career pathways and ability to earn an income that supports their financial independence.

Also, the emotional toll of abuse can have financial implications. Power and control dynamics can erode an individual's ability to assert themselves and set boundaries, especially if a victim has experienced chronic or long-term abuse. Abuse can distort a victim's or survivor's sense of identity and can create feelings of financial helplessness. Of course, financial dependence can also factor into a victim's decision to remain in an abusive relationship even long after they may wish to leave, and economic hardships can pose significant challenges after the relationship ends and along the abuse recovery journey.

Abusive relationships can be painful, traumatic experiences for victims and survivors. Any form of abuse can create challenges in the lives of victims and survivors. Understanding the dynamics of abusive relationships—especially the underlying power and control dynamics—is a helpful first step toward healing and recovery.

Although we know it can feel overwhelming to read about the harrowing experiences that victims and survivors often face, we want to end this chapter with a reminder that healing and recovery *are* possible. Later in this book, we will focus our attention more on the healing journey, including practical strategies survivors can use to support their healing and growth. Before we move into a focus on healing and recovery, we have one more chapter to cover to more fully explore the dynamics of abusive relationships. In Chapter 3, you'll find a deep dive into the topic of financial abuse. Read on to learn more about this specific form of abuse that many victims and survivors experience.

Chapter 3
Understanding Financial Abuse

In Chapter 2, we discussed the general dynamics of abusive relationships, and we saw that the common denominators in these relationships are the power and control dynamics. Abusers use many different types of tactics and behaviors to gain and maintain power over their victims. *Financial abuse* happens when abusers carry out their abusive actions in the arena of victims' and survivors' finances, and this includes other areas of life that are directly related to finances, such as career and educational pathways.

In this chapter, we'll do a deeper dive into the topic of financial abuse. By the end of this chapter, we hope you'll better understand the different forms financial abuse can take. If you've personally experienced any form of financial abuse, we hope this information will offer insights that can help you in your healing. We'll start by introducing five main categories of financial abuse:

1. Emotional, psychological, or verbal abuse with a financial focus
2. Financial control, isolation, and withholding
3. Deliberate, harmful, and potentially illegal financial acts
4. Interference with career and educational pathways
5. An "other" category reflecting each survivor's unique experiences. The "other" category is needed because some types of financial abuse don't fall neatly into one of the categories above.

These five categories of financial abuse show the complexity of the different layers and types of financially abusive behaviors. Often, survivors experience many types of financial abuse throughout their relationship, and financial abuse often co-occurs with other forms of abuse, like physical or sexual violence. Financial abuse can occur on a spectrum from less to more severe, but it's usually not too helpful to compare two people's experiences to try and decide who had it worse. It is, however, important is to understand your own unique experiences and how they're impacting you now.

Before we talk more about the categories of financial abuse, we want to start with an important disclaimer about how two partners in even healthy relationships can have differences in how they manage money, and financial differences between partners don't necessarily mean a relationship is financially abusive.

Defining Financial *Differences* in Healthy Relationships from Financial *Abuse* in Controlling Relationships

Healthy, non-abusive relationships can involve many different arrangements around financial decision-making and involvement in money matters. There are a lot of factors that impact how partners in couple relationships manage money. Some partners combine their finances into joint accounts, whereas other partners keep each person's money separate. Some people are naturally more interested in the topics of money and personal finance, whereas other people find the topic boring or confusing. Partners also may hold similar or different values and behaviors, such as around spending, saving, and valuing materialistic items. Recognizing and respecting these differences can help partners build a healthy, balanced partnership.

That said, building a shared sense of ownership, collaboration, and joint financial decision-making can help couples strengthen their relationships, even if partners don't combine their finances or one person does more of the day-to-day money management. That said, even in healthy relationships, we believe it's important for both partners to have access to information about the couple's finances, and this is true even if one person takes on more money management tasks. The potential risks of not being involved in family/relationship finances arise when we consider that life often takes unexpected turns, such as divorce, death, or severe illness. In these situations, a partner who has remained in the dark with no access or information about finances can find themselves in a vulnerable and precarious position. Even if both partners don't spend equal amounts of time and energy managing financial matters within the relationship, it's important for there to be a free flow of access and information so that nobody is left in an uninformed, vulnerable position if unexpected crises arise.

In contrast to healthy relationships in which both partners have access to financial information and resources in a mutually respected way, financial abuse occurs when one partner exerts undue control over financial matters. In the case of financial abuse, decisions are *not* jointly made, and money and finances become tools of abuse at the hands of the abuser. The victim may become more dependent on the abuser and vulnerable to further abuse because of their lack of access to financial resources. The victim lacks safety and freedom as a result of the abuser's financial restrictions.

When you read the information about financial abuse below, remember that just because financial responsibilities and tasks aren't managed exactly 50/50 in a relationship doesn't necessarily mean the relationship is harmful, risky, or abusive. In fact, across all shared aspects of life in long-term relationships, it's natural for each partner to take on more or less responsibility in certain areas, such as parenting or household tasks like cleaning. In healthy partnerships, partners find ways to divide tasks based on each person's preferences and strengths, even if the distribution isn't perfectly equal in every area of life. In contrast, in financially abusive relationships, pervasive power and control dynamics contribute to financial restrictions and harm to the victim or survivor. Financial abuse prevents victims from experiencing financial freedom because abusers exert power and control in this area of abusive relationships.

To summarize, the line that distinguishes healthy, natural differences between partners in healthy relationships and financially abusive dynamics relates to the absence or presence of power and control dynamics. In healthy relationships, differences are mutually agreed upon, and each partner is respected and valued. In abusive relationships, abusers unilaterally make decisions and impose their will around finances as a means of establishing control over their victims.

Understanding the Categories of Financial Abuse

Now that we've discussed the difference between financial differences in healthy relationships and financially abusive relationships, let's move into a detailed discussion of each category of financial abuse that we introduced above.

Emotional, psychological, or verbal abuse with a financial focus

In Chapter 2, we reviewed the dynamics of emotional, verbal, and psychological abuse. This section focuses on how these abuse tactics might play out in the context of victims' and survivors' finances. Abusers may use any of these forms of abuse—psychological, emotional, and verbal abuse—with a focus on hurting victims' and survivors' financial well-being.

Emotional financial abuse involves emotion-focused abusive tactics, with the intent of causing harm in the area of your finances. These tactics might include manipulating your emotions or exploiting your emotional vulnerabilities. For instance, an abuser might instill a sense of fear in you around financial matters by exaggerating how bad financial challenges are. This type of emotional fear-mongering might then lead you to feel more vulnerable, isolated, and dependent on the abuser. Another example of financially-focused emotional abuse involves an abuser manipulating your emotions so you'll feel pity, guilt, or sadness toward them and give them money that's rightfully yours. You might think of emotional financial abuse as your abuser's attempt to play with your emotions to gain control and undue influence over your finances.

Psychological financial abuse can show up in different forms, such as the mind-game aspects of gaslighting and manipulation we discussed in Chapter 2. For example, an abuser might intentionally try to create confusion about money matters by distorting the facts or trying to convince you that you don't understand your financial situation. Sometimes, abusers might claim that their harmful actions were, in fact, for the victim's well-being when clearly they are not. For example, imagine an abuser who opens a credit card in their victim's name without the victim's knowledge or consent, and then claims to have done this as a way to "help" the victim financially.

Verbal financial abuse involves using hurtful words and language aimed at undermining your confidence regarding finances. Abusers may use verbally abusive words to try to portray you as inadequate, foolish, or incompetent. Abusers' harmful words can lead you to feel inferior or that you lack intelligence about your financial situation. Ongoing verbal abuse can chip away at your self-worth, as the abuser's words inflict harm and negatively impact your self-perceptions about managing money.

More on financial gaslighting. Financial gaslighting can include elements of all three forms of abuse discussed in this section: psychological, emotional, and verbal abuse. We discussed gaslighting in Chapter 2, but because this term has become popularized in the media in recent years and it's an especially distressing form of financial abuse, we want to add a few more thoughts on this topic. Let's consider a hypothetical example to help illustrate how challenging financial gaslighting can be:

Jason and Maria have been married for three years and have two young children. Throughout their relationship, Jason has been emotionally and verbally abusive, and at times he has been physically violent toward Maria. The couple has faced some financial challenges, but Maria finally felt they were starting to get on the same page now that they've paid off their debts and are starting to save money for a down payment for their first home.

Jason told Maria a few months ago, "We'll work together to save up for this down payment. I agree this is a good goal for us so we can get into our first home as owners." For a little while, Jason seemed to be following through on his words, and the couple started to build up their savings. But secretly, Jason had his own self-serving plan. Several months into their family savings plan, Jason came home one day and told Maria he had taken money out of their savings account to use as a down payment to buy himself an expensive new car.

When Maria confronted Jason about how hurtful it was that he took joint money they were saving for a shared goal and used it for himself, without consulting her beforehand, Jason's reply was, "I never said I agreed to save together for a down payment." Maria knew she heard Jason say this, but she was confused because he seemed so certain when he denied it. Jason also added an additional guilt trip on Maria by saying she was being selfish and greedy for not supporting him in purchasing his dream car. Maria was left questioning whether she was in the wrong for questioning Jason's purchase.

As Maria's story shows, financial gaslighting can be confusing and harmful due to the betrayal involved. Financial gaslighting also can show up in abusers' actions, in addition to their deceitful words like those Jason used.

As another example, financial gaslighting also can happen when an abuser is secretive with their money, such as by hiding it or stashing it away in a private account that their partner doesn't have access to or know about—and this is not based on a mutually agreeable decision to keep their finances separate. In this kind of situation, it's tough for the victim to know exactly how much money the abuser actually makes or has in their account. If you've experienced this kind of financial gaslighting, you might have had a feeling that money was being kept secret or that things just weren't adding up regarding how your abuser was sharing information and financial resources with you. This was likely by design, with your abuser intentionally making it more difficult for you to figure out what was going on because they were covering their tracks and hiding information from you.

Abusers who gaslight by hiding money might use money secrets to control and confuse victims or survivors. When questions come up about money, abusers might try to make the other person feel guilty for asking, such as by saying, "If you trusted me, you wouldn't ask me questions like this." This mix of secrecy and deception with money can make things confusing and difficult for the person on the receiving end.

If you experienced financial gaslighting, your abuser may have used many tactics to confuse and hide information from you, so you may never have a full accounting of the financial picture within that relationship. However, we encourage you to trust your instincts if something feels off, especially if you asked questions that weren't answered clearly or you didn't even have "permission" to ask for more information. Learning to trust yourself again is often an important part of the healing journey for survivors who experienced gaslighting in their abusive relationships.

As we discussed earlier, the common thread in psychological, emotional, and verbally abusive behaviors—including gaslighting—is the abuser's pursuit of power and control. The motive behind a financial abuser's actions is to diminish their victim's self-esteem and create a sense of inadequacy and self-doubt around the victim's instincts and intuition. This calculated manipulation may lead victims to view their abusers as a figures of financial wisdom and to feel intimidated by their abuser's perceived financial know-how. This dynamic can happen in any abusive relationship, but it can be further compounded when abusers work in jobs involving financial expertise, such as in the accounting or financial advising fields. Abusers with jobs focusing on finances might leverage their professional status to further disregard and maintain control over their victims.

Abusers often use controlling tactics to increase their victims' financial dependence on them. A lot of people—whether or not they've faced abuse—struggle with self-confidence in the area of personal finances, especially because many of us lack much formal education about financial literacy. For this reason, victims and survivors may be especially vulnerable to abusers' manipulation and deceit when it comes to money, especially when abusers mix these tactics with verbal and emotional abuse that chips away at their self-esteem and confidence. In light of all of the dynamics that we mentioned throughout this section, the category of financially focused emotional, psychological, and verbal abuse can be an especially confusing, troubling, and impactful form of financial abuse.

Financial control, isolation, and withholding

The second category of financial abuse we'll cover in this chapter is financial control, isolation, and withholding. Again, it's important to understand this category of financial abuse within the context of the broader power and control dynamics that play out in abusive relationships.

The category of financial control, isolation, and withholding is especially relevant for survivors whose relationships involved combining their finances with their abusers (e.g., through marriage or cohabitation). Financial control tactics *can* occur when a couple is dating, such as if an abusive partner always makes the victim pay for dates. However, financial control, isolation, and withholding are generally more likely to occur when partners have some degree of combined or shared finances.

As we discussed earlier in this chapter, even in healthy relationships, partners might not be completely equally involved in financial issues within couple relationships. However, in instances of financial abuse, abusers *intentionally* restrict their partners' access to information and resources that significantly impact their economic well-being.

This can show up in many different ways. Abusers may altogether withhold information, denying their partners information and input into financial decisions. They might adopt a patronizing approach by providing a meager (and not mutually agreed upon) allowance or controlling victims' access to passwords, account numbers, and fund balances. Also, abusers may intentionally withhold their own financial contributions to the relationship, such as keeping their income secret. Abusers might withhold relevant financial information, exert complete control over financial matters, and intentionally keep their victims in the dark about the state of their finances.

Financial abuse can happen in relationships at all socioeconomic levels. An insightful book on the topic of abuse in higher-income relationships is *Not to People Like Us: Hidden Abuse in Upscale Marriages* by Susan Weitzman (2001). This book highlights the disparity between outward appearances of wealth and the hidden financial control in abusive relationships that can happen even at higher income levels. In such cases, a victim may appear to have it all. They might live in a luxurious home, drive an expensive car, and even have a high-paying job. However, within the confines of the abusive relationship, the reality is starkly different. Despite the appearance of a lavish lifestyle, the victim may have no access to any money. Their abuser might deliberately control everything, strategically keeping the victim away from financial resources, knowledge, and influence.

In more financially affluent situations with survivors, another issue that often arises is the perception that specific community resources, like domestic violence shelters, are not intended for survivors from higher-income brackets. Survivors from wealthier backgrounds might mistakenly believe that community resources are only available to people with lower household income levels. In truth, domestic violence services typically are available to *anyone* who has experienced an abusive relationship. Professionals working in these organizations are often trained to understand that abuse can happen in all segments of the community.

Financial abuse dynamics also may show up with abusers manipulating systems to financially harm their victims, which we'll discuss again later in this chapter. For instance, an abusive partner who controls all the finances might use those resources to hire an expensive lawyer for a child custody or divorce case, creating a significant financial disadvantage for the survivor with limited access to financial resources during legal proceedings. As such, we need to remember that survivors from all socioeconomic backgrounds can experience the negative repercussions of financial abuse, and this is especially true within the category of financial control, isolation, and withholding.

Here are some reflection questions that you can use to examine the extent to which your abuser may have used financial abuse tactics related to control, isolation, and withholding:

- *To what extent did your abuser exert sole control over financial decisions in your relationship?*

- *How often did you feel like your abuser treated you like a true, equal partner when it came to financial decision-making in your relationship?*

- *How often (if at all) did your abuser force you to justify or beg for money to make purchases, even ones that were essential for your family (e.g., groceries)?*

- *Were there specific instances in which your abuser blocked your access to financial resources or put you on an "allowance"? Consider if the allowance was mutually agreed upon or if the abuser made decisions about it unilaterally.*

- *In the context of your relationship, what was the balance of involvement in managing finances? Was this an arrangement you chose willfully, or was it forced upon you by your abuser?*

- *As you reflect on the relationship, do you feel that there were two sets of rules, expectations, or socio-economic statuses within your relationship/family?*

- *Were you intentionally kept in the dark about your finances? To what extent did you have access to information or shared financial resources involving your finances, even if you weren't as directly involved in managing the finances as your partner was?*

- *Were you denied access to passwords, account numbers, or financial documents?*

- *Did your abuser withhold information about income, expenses, or financial plans?*

- *Were any of your needs or wants that you could have theoretically afforded withheld from you as a form of control or punishment?*

Overall, the controlling, isolating, and withholding dynamics involved in financial abuse can show up in many harmful ways. These tactics not only create significant hurdles for victims attempting to leave an abusive relationship, but they also can make it harder to thrive financially and achieve a sense of financial well-being post-separation. Recognizing these patterns can offer important insights for survivors along the pathway to economic recovery and independence.

Deliberate, harmful, and potentially illegal financial acts

In this section, we explore a particularly insidious and harmful form of financial abuse—deliberate, harmful, and potentially illegal financial acts that abusers may use to gain and sustain power and control over their partners.

This form of financial abuse can happen in many different ways and lead to significant consequences for survivors. If you suspect you've been subjected to this form of financial abuse, we recommend you consider seeking individualized advice, such as from law enforcement, a lawyer, or a victim advocate. This is especially important if you believe your abuser's actions may have involved illegal or criminal acts. While this section covers the general dynamics of these forms of financial abuse, we suggest you consult with an appropriately trained professional about your specific situation, especially if legal concerns arise.

Throughout our years working with survivors of domestic violence, we've heard many horrific stories of abusers resorting to severe measures to directly harm survivors in the area of their finances. Examples of the types of abusive actions we've heard include the following: engaging in fraud and deception, purposely sabotaging victims' credit, exploiting systems and inflicting related costs, and engaging in financially abusive parenting-related tactics when children are involved. Let's look at each of these tactics individually.

Fraudulent or deceptive actions. One form of fraud and deception occurs when abusers steal from their partners. This could involve the abuser insisting that, upon receiving their paycheck, the victim must turn over all or part of it to the abuser. Another example of theft might occur without the partner's knowledge or consent, such as directly taking money from a purse or wallet or withdrawing funds from an account for personal use without permission.

Another form of fraudulent or deceptive actions involves identity theft or fraud, particularly in longer-term relationships in which an abuser gains access to personal information, such as your Social Security Number, birth date, address, and passwords to bank accounts. In these cases, an abuser might open a bank account or credit card in a survivor's name without consent. Alternatively, they may use the survivor's information to commit fraud against someone else or run a scam. Given the potential legal implications of this type of financial abuse, seeking legal advice is advisable if you experienced something like this.

The dynamics of intimate relationships often involve sharing more personal information, resources, and accounts as partners become closer, even in healthy relationships. However, in an abusive relationship, this heightened closeness can create vulnerability, especially when dealing with an abuser who has demonstrated a lack of concern for your overall well-being.

Damaging your credit. Abusers may intentionally act in ways that leave their victims in a bad place regarding debt or credit. Some of these actions may fall under fraudulent activities, such as taking out debt without their partner's consent or knowledge. Other efforts to destroy a survivor's credit can occur, such as co-signing on a loan and then failing to repay it, leading to potential consequences for the survivor's credit records.

Exploiting systems. Abusers might seek to inflict financial harm by exploiting social systems and their associated costs for victims or survivors. The exploitation of systems is often a power play for control, harassment, and verbal abuse, and this can result in significant financial costs for survivors. In particular, abusers who hold a stronger financial position than their victims often use their privileged status within these systems, including leveraging their more significant financial resources to their advantage.

One example of exploiting systems involves carrying out legal abuse through court systems, such as engaging in frivolous custody battles and civil and criminal court processes. Abusers' deliberate manipulation of legal systems can be expensive and significantly impact victims' and survivors' financial well-being.

Abusers also may attempt to exploit systems by making false accusations to Child Protective Services. Additionally, abusers might try to exploit systems by spreading lies, damaging survivors' reputations, and creating added costs and hurdles for survivors to navigate. In the next section, we'll also look at how abusers may exploit workplace systems for similar purposes.

Abusers who have systematically controlled their victims' access to financial resources throughout the relationship often have more financial means to hire professionals, such as lawyers, to help them exploit systems to carry out abuse. (We will add a note that we do not believe all lawyers are bad! Many lawyers are fierce advocates for survivors' rights, and others may be duped by abusers' lies and manipulation and unknowingly play into abusers' power and control tactics.)

Survivors face many potential challenges when they are contending with vindictive abusers who have access to substantially greater financial resources. Many of the systems that abusers exploit lack a trauma-informed, supportive approach for survivors. When an abuser exploits systems to carry out abuse, survivors can face many negative impacts on their finances, as well as other areas of their lives, such as added layers of emotional trauma.

Parenting-related financial abuse. The final category of deliberately harmful, and potentially illegal, financial acts we'll cover here involves parenting-related actions when children are involved. For instance, abusers may make financial threats related to parenting, such as if they warn victims that if they leave the relationship, they won't provide any financial support for their children.

Abusers might also intimidate survivors by stating their intent to use legal systems to prevent access to the children. Also, abusers might refuse to fulfill their obligations in paying child support or other costs related to the children, a situation that could require legal intervention that survivors may not be able to afford.

Unfortunately, there are many types of deliberate, harmful actions abusers may take to inflict financial harm on victims and survivors. Because this form of financial abuse can be so nuanced, your experiences might differ from the examples covered in this section. If you've faced this form of financial abuse, consider seeking guidance from law enforcement, a lawyer, a victim advocate, or other specialists in your area to assess your experiences and determine if legal or criminal actions can be pursued.

Interference with career and educational pathways that impact survivors' financial well-being

Another way abusers can harm victims' and survivors' financial well-being is by interfering with their career or educational pathways. Because academic and career paths are so closely tied to survivors' economic well-being, abusers' attempts to interfere in these areas can be considered a form of financial abuse. Later in this book in Chapter 9, we'll also explore how the process of recovering from abuse—especially in the area of your finances—might involve seeking out new opportunities in your career or education.

Abusers often use power and control tactics to try to derail victims' and survivors' careers and educational pursuits. Career-related abuse can show up in different ways based on survivors' career paths and work environments. Here are a few examples of how abusers may undermine survivors' successes at work:

First, abusers may engage in emotional or psychological abuse to belittle survivors' career paths or specific work-related goals. Christine experienced this firsthand and shares the following brief story:

> *I was in the middle of working toward a significant goal that I'd wanted to work on for years. When it finally came time for me to work on it, I told my abuser about it and hoped he*

would share in my excitement. Instead, he put the idea down, dismissed its significance, and suggested that it wouldn't make any difference in the world even if it came to pass. I was so hurt by his harsh words and lack of support. Thankfully, however, I chose not to let those words stop me from pursuing my goal, and I actually achieved my goal. I guess he was wrong after all!

This little anecdote is a good reminder that, just because an abuser says something hurtful in an attempt to make a victim feel small, this does not mean it's true! Even still, harsh criticisms and harmful comments can get into your mind, leading you to lose confidence in your ability to achieve your dreams. If your confidence is lacking, you might abandon your career goals altogether if your partner, who you hope would be your biggest supporter, puts your goals down.

Abusers' harsh criticisms and hurtful comments can impact your self-esteem and progress in your career. If your sense of self-worth is deeply affected, you might be tempted to abandon your career goals altogether, especially if you feel overwhelmed by your abuser's negativity and lack of support. The consequences of an abusive relationship also can affect survivors' careers when ongoing abusive processes, such as frivolous court cases, arise. Survivors may need to miss work frequently to attend court dates, and repeated work absences can put their jobs at risk and harm their financial well-being.

Another way abusers may interfere with survivors' career pathways is through career-related isolation and control. This could involve not allowing a survivor not to go to work or, as we mentioned earlier, coercing them to surrender their paychecks to the abuser. Abusers may also restrict survivors' career choices. Here, we're not discussing situations where one partner willingly chooses to be a stay-at-home parent or homemaker or to make other career sacrifices on behalf of their family life. Instead, we're addressing cases in which an abuser limits their victim's career options to exert control and foster dependence.

Similar dynamics also can show up in survivors' educational pathways. Once again, we might find abusers preventing their partners from pursuing their academic goals. Or, abusers might show up and harass their partners in the classroom, follow them from class to class, or restrict their ability to work with classmates on required group projects.

Abusers also may be psychologically or emotionally abusive to undermine their victims' confidence in reaching their educational goals. Below, you'll find another hypothetical case example to illustrate this type of financial abuse:

After five years of being a stay-at-home mother to her son, Monica is interested in returning to work now that her son is starting kindergarten. Monica's husband, Theo, has a long history of being controlling and verbally, emotionally, and physically abusive toward her. Theo immediately disapproved when Monica told him about her interest in returning to school to get her Master's degree so she could refresh her professional training and prepare to re-enter the accounting field. He made disparaging comments, such as saying that she wouldn't be smart enough to be successful in graduate school. He also said with a hostile tone in his voice, "You can go back to school if you want to, but don't expect me to change my work schedule to watch our boy while you're off chasing this ridiculous dream."

Overall, as Monica's situation illustrates, there are many possible ways in which your abuser may have inflicted harm on your career and educational pathways, which can lead to damaging consequences in your overall financial well-being. Whether by derailing you from pursuing goals, hindering your success at work or in education, or deliberately harassing, disparaging, or slandering you—there are many ways you may have experienced significant impacts of financial abuse within your work life and in pursuit of your educational goals.

The "other" category: Forms of financial abuse that are unique to you

We include this last "other" category of financial abuse because every survivor's experiences of abuse are unique and nuanced. After reading through all the categories and examples of financial abuse described above, you may find that some resonated with you while others didn't quite match your experiences. You also may have faced unique situations that don't fit neatly into one of the above-mentioned categories. If you've experienced any degree of abuse impacting your finances, please remember that your experiences are valid, even if they don't neatly fit into any of the categories mentioned above.

We invite you to take a moment to reflect on the various categories of financial abuse we discussed throughout this chapter and consider how your experiences may or may not align with those categories. If your experiences fall outside these categories, this "other" category provides the space to validate your unique experiences and recognize the unique ways that financial abuse played out in your life.

Each person's life experiences are unique, so permit yourself to define your experiences in ways that are meaningful to you without getting too caught up in a need to fit them into formal definitions or categories. What's most important is honoring your unique experiences and committing to ongoing healing from any forms of abuse you faced that continue to impact your life today.

Important Messages if You Have Faced Financial Abuse

This chapter highlighted how financial abuse can show up in many ways in abusive relationships. Each type of financial abuse can be harmful and have detrimental effects on survivors' lives and economic well-being. The effects of financial abuse also often interact with the consequences of other forms of abuse, such as physical, emotional, psychological, or sexual abuse. Recognizing the complexity of these interactions helps us to understand more fully the potential impacts of abuse on survivors.

All the potential dynamics and consequences of abuse add to the complexity of the healing process for survivors. As we move forward to the following chapters of this book, we'll shift our focus to offering tools, resources, and information to support your recovery from past abuse, including recovering from the financial consequences you're facing. Before we move on, here are a few important messages and reminders for anyone who has faced financial abuse.

First and foremost, remember the abuse is not your fault. You did not deserve to be mistreated, including in the area of your finances. Regardless of how much knowledge and confidence you have (or don't have) around financial matters, your abuser is 100% responsible for their harmful actions. Remind yourself as often as needed that they are fully accountable for their actions, and resist the temptation to blame yourself for the harm caused by this other person.

Second, know that you are not alone. Many survivors, including the two of us as authors of this book, have experienced financial abuse in our own lives. Recognizing that financial abuse is a common occurrence in abusive relationships is an important step. You are not alone, and there is no need to feel ashamed of your experiences. We encourage you to move forward in your recovery process without shame, and we dive deeper into this topic in Chapter 5.

Next, healing is possible. Remember that you can recover from financial abuse and other forms of abuse that have impacted your life and finances. The journey toward recovery, including overcoming financial abuse, can be lengthy and complex, but strive to hold onto hope that healing is within your reach. You have the strength to heal, recover, and envision a brighter future in all aspects of your life, including your finances.

Finally, know that help is available. Legal, financial advisory, mental health, and other resources may offer valuable support to you as you navigate the financial and broader aftermath of the abuse you experienced. In upcoming chapters, we'll explore various types of resources that may be helpful. For now, remember that seeking help is a brave step to take, and you are worthy of having positive, encouraging, and knowledgeable supporters in your corner.

It *is* possible to build a solid financial foundation for your life, regardless of where you are starting from now. You can do this. Many survivors have taken on the brave journey from having virtually nothing to thriving in their finances, and you *can* achieve this as well. While it might seem daunting at the moment, and it may take some time before you can bring your vision of financial well-being to reality, there is hope for a brighter future for your life. Our aim for the remainder of this book is to provide you with encouragement, tools, and information to support you in taking steps from experiencing abuse toward recovery and ultimately toward thriving in your finances and your life overall.

Chapter 4

Financial Recovery as Part of the Overall Healing Journey from an Abusive Relationship

Healing from an abusive relationship is a journey toward hope and restoration in all areas of our lives. While this book focuses on financial abuse recovery, it's important to remember that financial healing is deeply interwoven with other dimensions of recovery—including our mental and emotional well-being, interpersonal relationships, and connections to our broader community.

In this chapter, we describe the Pathways for Supporting Survivors Model that Christine developed to offer a framework for understanding the overall long-term healing journey for survivors of abusive relationships (Murray, 2024a). We include applications of this framework for recovery in the area of financial well-being.

For many survivors, financial freedom and well-being are essential aspects of the healing process. Our personal and professional experiences have shown us that financial well-being is often a key to securing a better quality of life for survivors and, if applicable, their children or families. Financial consequences of abuse often entrap survivors in unsafe situations, and so financial autonomy can become a powerful tool for breaking free and establishing a life that is full of safety, freedom, and self-determination. By regaining control over our finances, we lay the groundwork for a future where we feel empowered, secure, and in charge of our destiny.

Below are a few examples of how financial freedom can help survivors reshape their lives in meaningful ways:

• Financial well-being reduces the likelihood of returning to an abusive situation out of necessity and dependence on an abuser. It can provide a safety net to help prevent re-entry into harmful relationships.

• The stress of financial troubles and the fear associated with being trapped in an abusive relationship can take a significant toll on survivors' mental health. Financial well-being can alleviate this stress and contribute to emotional healing and empowerment. It also opens up energy and space to focus on things you love.

• Developing financial literacy and skills can help rebuild self-confidence that was eroded by an abusive relationship. Working toward financial goals affirms your ability to take care of yourself and, if applicable, your family.

• Financial well-being can open doors to new opportunities and choices, allowing you to rebuild your life on your terms, not restricted by the constraints and fear imposed by an abuser. For example, financial resources might provide you with opportunities to find stable housing, pursue further education, or even launch a new business venture.

• As we discussed earlier, making progress toward financial goals can be a more concrete and tangible arena for tracking your progress than other more intangible aspects of healing, such as building your self-esteem and trusting yourself more. By setting financial goals and tracking your progress, you can build momentum and confidence in your ability to create positive changes in your life.

Focusing on financial well-being can be an important part of the healing journey for many survivors. Because you decided to read this book, we suspect that financial recovery is one priority for you along your recovery process. At the same time, know that it is okay if other aspects of your healing journey are a higher priority in your life, at least at this point in time. As you read this chapter, take time to reflect on how much of a priority your financial well-being is as part of your healing journey. It may be that you'd find it more useful to focus on other aspects of your healing (e.g., your mental health or recovering from a physical injury) first, and then wait to focus more on your finances at a later time. Always remember that your journey is your own, and you can move at your own pace and address your goals in the order that makes sense to you.

The Pathway for Supporting Survivors Model: 6 Commitments Along the Healing Journey

For many survivors of abusive relationships, the long-term healing journey in the aftermath of abuse is a lengthy, confusing, and complicated one. Perhaps because the overall issues of domestic violence and other forms of relationship abuse have only relatively recently become more visible in communities (and there is still a long way to go in this area!), guidance for the healing process is often limited. Survivors frequently feel they are navigating a winding road without a map or clear destination.

Recognizing the need for more guidance for survivors along the healing journey, Christine recently launched The Source for Survivors (www.sourceforsurvivors.info), an online resource for survivors and their community supporters. The Source for Survivors is grounded in the Pathway for Supporting Survivors Model (Murray, 2023; Murray, 2024), which outlines 6 Commitments that can guide the path to healing. These 6 Commitments are as follows:

1. Being Intentional
2. Prioritizing Safety
3. Taking a Long-Range View
4. Making Steps Forward
5. Reflecting
6. *Paying it Forward (*This commitment is always optional for survivors.)

The 6 Commitments are not intended to be viewed as a rigid, prescriptive set of steps to follow. In other words, survivors don't need to master being intentional first before moving on to prioritizing their safety second, and so on. Instead, the 6 Commitments are meant to be ongoing, overlapping processes that survivors can prioritize along the healing journey to provide support, reassurance, and tangible areas of focus to support their progress.

Each of the 6 Commitments in the Pathways for Supporting Survivors Model can be applied to survivors and community supporters. For the purposes of this book, we'll explore the 6 Commitments for survivors through the lens of healing from financial abuse. We include a few self-reflection questions for each Commitment to explore how each commitment applies to your life now.

Commitment 1: Being Intentional

The first commitment is Being Intentional. This commitment reflects the importance of being proactive and dedicated to our healing processes. You've probably heard the saying, "Time heals all wounds." However, this is not necessarily true when it comes to healing the hurts and potential traumatic effects of having been in an abusive relationship. Survivors can enhance their healing journey by bringing intentionality and focus to it. The passing of time can help alleviate some pains, but time alone often is not sufficient to bring about the fullness of healing that many survivors desire.

Being intentional about your financial recovery while healing emotionally can be challenging, but it is possible. Gaining clarity about your financial goals is a great place to start. Exploring connections between your emotional healing and your journey toward financial well-being is also important. Fostering a mindset that creates intentional space for your healing can serve as a stepping stone toward feeling empowered and capable. Creating daily routines to put your intentional mindset into practice helps build confidence through consistent practice. And, being intentional about surrounding yourself with supportive people helps validate your strengths and move you forward on this journey.

Self-reflection questions for Commitment 1:

● *What does being intentional about your healing process look like to you?*

● *What are your reactions to the saying, "Time heals all wounds," in the context of healing from an abusive relationship?*

● *What barriers do you face that make it challenging to bring intentionality to your healing journey? Examples could include financial hardships that make it more difficult to access potentially helpful services (e.g., counseling), a hectic schedule, or a lack of social support.*

Commitment 2: Prioritizing Safety

Your safety, both physical and emotional, is central to every aspect of your recovery journey. Commitment 2, Prioritizing Safety, is critical to rebuilding your life, whether you're still facing threats from your abuser or if you're no longer in direct contact with them. Prioritizing safety means making decisions that protect you from further harm and support your overall well-being. Safety means being safe from physical harm, and it also relates to feeling psychologically and emotionally secure. It includes being free from verbal and emotional abuse and feeling safe from manipulation, intimidation, and coercion. Prioritizing safety is about creating an environment in which you can thrive physically and emotionally without feeling threats of further harm or distress.

Emotional safety also means expressing yourself without fear of judgment or retaliation and having the emotional and mental space to heal and grow. This also includes pacing yourself, developing coping skills, and practicing self-care to avoid overwhelm and protect your well-being. Whether you support your safety by establishing boundaries, seeking safe environments, or engaging in practices that foster your emotional resilience, Commitment 2 underscores the importance of creating a safe context for your healing.

Another critical aspect of ensuring your safety—especially if you still face any safety risks related to the abuse—is having a well-thought-out safety plan. If you're considering leaving or are in the process of leaving an abusive relationship, it's important to note that this is often the most dangerous time for a victim. The shift in power away from the abuser can lead to an escalation in their harmful behaviors. For assistance and support in developing a personalized safety plan for you, consider contacting national or local resources like the National Domestic Violence Hotline (https://www.thehotline.org/) or a victim services agency to connect with a trained professional. Visit this book's website at www.sourceforsurvivors.info/financialabuse for more information about how to connect with resources.

Striving for a sense of financial safety and security also can be an important dimension of financial abuse recovery. Financial security can contribute to your overall sense of safety and security in life. As applied to your finances, Commitment 2 might involve protecting your financial assets, such as securing your bank accounts, monitoring your credit report, or establishing an emergency fund. Financial recovery also may include creating a long-term plan to rebuild your credit or address debts that were accumulated during the abusive relationship. Prioritizing financial safety also means protecting your economic autonomy as you heal. For survivors of financial abuse, it may also involve carefully navigating financial decisions to avoid further exploitation. Prioritizing a sense of financial safety empowers you to rebuild your financial life in a way that safeguards your well-being and supports your recovery.

A safe environment empowers us to make confident financial decisions without fear of criticism or manipulation. Abuse, including financial abuse, can leave survivors feeling powerless and unworthy. When you feel physically and psychologically safe, you can rebuild your self-esteem, regain confidence in managing your finances, and make self-directed decisions that support your financial well-being. This sense of safety can help you restore a sense of control over your life and finances, enabling you to transition from merely surviving to thriving and healing richer.

Self-reflection questions for Commitment 2:

- *What does safety mean to you? What does the concept of financial safety and security look like to you?*

- *What does a safe environment look and feel like to you?*

- *Where can you connect with healthy, safe sources of support along your healing journey?*

Commitment 3: Taking a Long-Range View

Healing from an abusive relationship is a process that unfolds over time, and keeping a big-picture mindset can help you navigate the ups and downs along the way. Commitment 3, Taking a Long-Range View, encourages you to practice patience and resilience, acknowledging that recovery usually isn't a straight line from Point A (the abuse) to Point B (complete healing). Rather, growth can continue throughout your life. Patience is helpful as you celebrate your wins, no matter how small, while maintaining your long-term goals for personal development and healing. By keeping your eyes on long-term healing, you can celebrate day-to-day successes while understanding that your overall healing journey will probably take a while.

Regarding financial recovery, adopting a long-range view helps you remain patient and focused on your broader financial goals. Rebuilding financial health after abuse may take months or years, and adopting a long-term perspective can help survivors navigate the discouragements they feel over time. Celebrate small victories, such as paying down debts or saving more for the future. Focus on building long-term financial stability rather than seeking quick fixes, knowing that it's okay to take the time you need to reach your long-term goals.

Seeking immediate financial relief may be necessary to focus on right now—such as if you need access to food, affordable housing, or child care. When the timing is right for you, you can also begin to plan for your future, whether that involves saving for retirement, investing in further education, or building wealth. Understanding that financial recovery is a marathon, not a sprint, allows you to make informed decisions that can lead to lasting financial stability and independence. It just might take some time to get there.

Starting over after an abusive relationship can feel overwhelming. It's not just about rebuilding your finances—it's also about healing from the lasting emotional and psychological effects of the abuse. It's natural to experience grief, fear, and frustration during this journey, and processing these feelings in healthy ways is an important part of the healing process.

Recovery looks different for everyone. You may be starting from scratch, struggling with unmet basic needs like housing and food, or dealing with the impacts of damaged credit. These challenges are real and can feel daunting, but know that you can move toward hope and financial well-being. Progress may be slow, and setbacks are likely to happen. However, practicing patience and celebrating your victories can help you maintain your momentum and build confidence. While the journey might be challenging, it's also a reflection of your strength and resilience that you are embracing this process. With each step you take toward rebuilding your financial life and working on other healing aspects, remember that you are reclaiming your power and creating your future on your terms.

Self-reflection questions for Commitment 3:

- *In general, would you describe yourself as a more patient or impatient person? How might this impact your healing experiences if you start to feel like you are taking a long time to move forward?*

- *What are some ways you can provide comfort and encouragement to yourself when you feel overwhelmed or frustrated along your healing journey?*

- *Who do you know that you might look at as an inspiration or role model for being patient and enduring long-lasting challenges in life? What can you learn from their experiences?*

Commitment 4: Making Steps Forward

Moving forward on the path to recovery involves taking deliberate, actionable steps toward your vision of what healing and recovery mean to you. Commitment 4, Making Steps Forward, emphasizes the importance of progress, no matter how small, and encourages survivors to focus on practical strategies that move them closer to their healing goals.

Even when the journey feels unclear, every small step forward brings you closer to healing. It's not necessary to tackle every aspect of your life at once. Instead, focus on specific areas where you feel ready and able to make changes. Whether seeking support or developing new habits, Commitment 4 is about prioritizing intentional action, while remembering that resting is a powerful form of action as well. In other words, sometimes the steps we most need to take involve taking breaks to rest and recharge. By prioritizing these steps and allowing yourself the grace to move at your own pace, you can steadily advance on your path to recovery.

Consistent, deliberate actions are also helpful for pursuing financial well-being and recovery. Whether you're opening a savings account, creating a budget, or negotiating debt repayment, each step forward contributes to your overall financial health. Small, manageable financial steps, such as reviewing your credit report, setting up an emergency fund, or attending financial education workshops, can lead to meaningful progress. Celebrate even the most seemingly minor financial victories, like sticking to a budget or avoiding an impulsive purchase. These steps build momentum and confidence, helping you regain control of your financial future one decision at a time.

The specific, deliberate steps forward that each survivor needs will vary, and each person's needs also will shift and change over time. Sometimes, you may want to focus on several goals at once, while at other times, you might need to focus all your attention and energy on one big goal. Below, we provide a few common meaningful steps forward that often resonate with survivors along the healing journey, including connecting with supportive resources, setting and maintaining boundaries, practicing positive self-talk and self-compassion, and working toward personally meaningful goals and changes. Keep in mind, however, that these are just examples of the types of forward steps that may be part of the healing process, and other steps may be more relevant in your life than the examples described below.

Connecting with supportive resources. Lean into the support available to you from various sources. You may find it helpful to connect with your local domestic violence agency or the National Domestic Violence Hotline, where professionals are trained to support victims and survivors of abuse. Additionally, seek support from trusted loved ones and your community who can provide emotional and practical assistance. As you take steps in specific areas of your financial life, such as your career path, consider exploring resources like community-based nonprofits or community colleges, which may offer job training programs to help you rebuild your financial independence. We'll discuss career and educational goals further in Chapter 9.

You may benefit from seeking consumer credit counseling if you need help managing debt, but choose credible, nonprofit resources. Additionally, seek free community or online financial education resources to boost your financial knowledge. Chapter 8 will provide more information on potential sources of support related to financial goals.

At times, you may need to reach out for urgent help, such as during the time of leaving an abusive relationship. There's no shame in reaching out for help to promote your well-being and safety, such as staying with a safe person(s) or at a domestic violence shelter temporarily while you get back on your feet. Remember, the support you need is out there, and reaching out is a sign of strength, not weakness.

Don't hesitate to ask for help when you need it, although we acknowledge that sometimes the process of seeking help can be frustrating. You may not always connect with helpful sources of support right away, so be persistent and remember that you are worthy of surrounding yourself with a network of supportive resources at all stages of your healing journey.

Setting and maintaining boundaries. Boundaries are essential limits we set with others to protect our emotional, mental, and physical well-being. This section highlights steps survivors can take to establish boundaries, particularly with abusers, but also with others who may negatively impact their lives, such as hostile coworkers or unsupportive family members. Establishing healthy boundaries can support all aspects of survivors' healing, and there also can be financial benefits. These could include minimizing further financial damages as much as possible and limiting access to people (including your abuser) who may try to cause you further financial harm.

Setting boundaries with an abuser is challenging due to their typical patterns of boundary crossings. In some cases, seeking help from law enforcement or domestic violence agencies may be necessary, especially if a restraining order is needed. Going "no contact," when possible, is a powerful boundary that involves cutting off all forms of communication with someone who has shown you time and again that they are intent on causing you harm. This isn't always feasible, especially if children are involved. However, where it is possible to cut off contact with abusers, going no contact can help to create space for healing. Steps to going no contact might include blocking the abuser on social media, email, and phone, as well as closing any shared accounts.

Even if going completely no contact is not an option, it is helpful to strive to establish emotional and physical boundaries as much as possible. Emotional boundaries help you maintain a healthy distance from an unsafe person, protecting yourself from their belittling behavior and criticisms. Practicing detachment, where you remind yourself that the abuser's actions reflect their issues, not yours, can be another powerful tool for setting emotional boundaries. Prepare boundary-setting statements, like "If you continue to speak to me this way, I will end the conversation," to assert your limits, but always be mindful of any potential safety risks if this type of statement might increase the risk your abuser would retaliate against you. Again here, we recommend developing a safety plan with support from a trained professional to address any safety concerns. (See this book's website at www.sourceforsurvivors.info/financialabuse for resources if you face ongoing safety risks).

Physical boundaries also are useful as a way to implement safeguards for your personal space, body, and privacy. Decide how to respond if these boundaries are crossed, such as leaving the situation or seeking help from a crisis hotline or emergency services. Consistently enforcing boundaries is important for promoting your safety. If you must be around the abuser, aim to stay in public areas or where others are present, and avoid being alone in confined spaces. If enforcing physical boundaries could lead to harm, prioritize your safety, even if it means leaving the situation, calling a crisis hotline for support, involving law enforcement, or developing a safety plan as we discussed above.

Practicing positive self-talk and self-compassion. Paying attention to your self-talk and integrating self-compassion into your daily life can help you navigate the negative thoughts that may feel paralyzing to you. It's important to recognize that negative self-talk often stems from experiences of abuse and is not a reflection of your ability to heal and succeed. Embracing self-compassion can help you cultivate a healthier, more realistic mindset.

In Eileen's private practice, where she works primarily with survivors of abusive relationships, fostering self-compassion is a key aspect of the therapeutic process. Dr. Kristin Neff's (n.d.) research highlights that self-compassion is one of the most powerful tools for coping and building resilience, and practicing self-compassion can significantly improve our mental and emotional well-being. Becoming more self-compassionate helps motivate us to make changes and reach our goals, not because we feel inadequate, but because we care about ourselves and want to be happy.

Integrating self-compassion into regular routines helps survivors care for the emotional wounds left by abuse, gradually softening the harsh inner voice that may linger from those experiences. This practice is valuable for making progress toward our healing goals. By allowing self-compassion to guide us, we can pause and acknowledge our humanity during difficult emotions, enabling these feelings to flow through us instead of remaining stuck and causing ongoing distress. For practical guidance, Dr. Kristin Neff offers audio self-compassion practices and other resources on her website, self-compassion.org.

Working toward personally meaningful goals and changes. Your healing journey is deeply personal, and your unique needs and experiences can guide your steps forward. Most importantly, focus on actions that resonate with you, knowing that your priorities may shift over time. Initially, your efforts may center on securing stability in your daily life, ensuring your basic needs are met, and creating a foundation for starting to rebuild your life. As you move forward, building your financial and emotional well-being might involve working to increase your financial resources, developing new knowledge or skills, or seeking the support of professionals and loved ones.

As you begin to heal, you may find it empowering to gain knowledge in areas that strengthen your independence—financial, emotional, or otherwise. Setting goals that reflect your personal hopes and dreams, and then working toward those goals at your own pace is a key to reclaiming your power and shaping your future. Ultimately, this journey is about more than just recovery; it's about thriving in a meaningful and sustainable way. Each step you take is a testament to your resilience and strength, guiding you toward a life that aligns with your values and dreams. You may not yet feel like you totally know what those values and dreams are, which is not an unusual experience for people who have faced abusive relationships. Stay tuned for Chapter 7, which will focus on helping you to envision goals and dreams for your future.

Self-reflection questions for Commitment 4:

● *What small, manageable goals do you wish to set and work toward at this moment in time? You can set goals with timelines that are as long or short as you'd like. Even just a goal for today (or maybe just the next hour) is plenty!*

● *What healthy supports and resources can you access to help you move toward these goals?*

● *What daily routines can you put in place to help keep you on track toward reaching your goals?*

● *How can you practice self-compassion as you navigate your healing journey and move toward financial well-being?*

Commitment 5: Reflecting

Commitment 5, Reflecting, is a powerful tool for assessing what's working and what you'd like to be different along your healing journey.

Making time for regular self-reflection provides you with opportunities to assess your progress, celebrate your successes, and learn from the challenges you've faced. By regularly reflecting on your journey, you can gain valuable insights into what needs adjustment and how far you've come. Commitment 5 helps ensure that your recovery is not just about moving forward, but it's also about deepening your understanding of yourself in the process.

Self-reflection is valuable for those of us who have experienced abuse, as it allows us to reconnect with our emotions, thoughts, and physical well-being. It's natural for those who have experienced abuse to shift their focus outward from their own experiences, often leading to a hyper-awareness of others' moods and behaviors at the expense of our own needs. Mindful self-reflection helps to shift that focus inward, empowering us to make intentional choices that prioritize our well-being rather than reacting out of fear or habit.

Financial self-reflection involves regularly reviewing your progress to identify steps you're taking that are helping you regain control of your finances. Whether it's by assessing how well your budgeting strategy is working or by recognizing where you might need more support, ongoing reflection helps you stay aligned with your financial goals. By reflecting on your financial progress, you can celebrate milestones, identify areas for improvement, and reinforce your commitment to achieving financial well-being.

Throughout this book, we've provided many self-reflection questions to help you explore how your experiences have shaped your thoughts and behaviors. These kinds of questions offer examples of topics for reflecting on your motivations, values, emotions, goals, and values related to your finances. They also offer opportunities to learn from your decisions, both financial and emotional, building confidence in your ability to navigate your journey with intention and resilience.

By integrating reflection into your routine, you stay attuned to your progress and gain valuable insights to help guide you toward a life that reflects your values and dreams.

Self-reflection questions for Commitment 5:

- *How do you feel about your financial future, and what fears or anxieties do you want to address?*

- *How easy or difficult do you typically find it to be to engage in deep self-reflection?*

- *What types of self-reflection strategies work best for you? Examples might include journaling, meditation, meeting with a professional counselor, or bouncing your ideas with a trusted friend or family member.*

Commitment 6: *Paying it Forward (*This commitment is always optional for survivors.)

While entirely optional, many survivors find meaning in their healing journeys by supporting others on a similar path. Supporting others takes many forms, whether through advocacy, raising awareness, or simply being a compassionate listener. If and when you feel ready, giving back can help to offer a sense of purpose and meaning from your experiences with abuse. For survivors interested in giving back to others along their healing journey, Commitment 6, Paying it Forward, is about using your experiences to uplift others while reinforcing your growth and resilience.

In the context of financial recovery, paying it forward might involve offering support to others who are struggling with financial abuse, sharing knowledge you've gained about financial literacy, or even making financial or volunteer contributions to a local domestic violence agency. Whether through community involvement, mentoring, or advocating for policies that protect survivors, helping others navigate their abuse recovery journey can be a rewarding way to use your experience for good. Giving back also can serve as a reminder of your strength and progress toward financial empowerment.

If Commitment 6, Paying it Forward, resonates with you—now or in the future—here are some ways you might use your experiences to support others:

Sharing your story. Sharing your personal story can help to raise awareness about abuse and reduce stigma, encouraging others to seek help. Deciding to share your story publicly is a deeply personal decision that requires careful consideration of your emotional and physical safety. Before you consider going public with your story, ensure you feel grounded, supported, and ready to take on that vulnerable way of opening up to others. You may also want to consider sharing your story anonymously or within a supportive community as alternative, less public ways of sharing your story.

Some potential opportunities for sharing your story include public speaking at awareness events, writing a blog post based on your experiences and insights, or even simply telling your story to someone in your life who is also impacted by an abusive relationship. Of course, remember that you are not under any obligation to share your story with anyone you don't want to share it with, now or at any point in the future. Empower yourself to decide whether, when, and how telling your story might feel safe and meaningful to you.

Peer support. Examples of peer support include facilitating support groups or providing one-on-one assistance. Leading or participating in a support group can help create a safe space for survivors to share experiences and feel validated within a community. Offering one-on-one support can also be a powerful and empowering way to help others. Often, it is helpful (and perhaps even required) to receive appropriate training and to ensure you are in a healthy, safe emotional position along your healing journey before taking on these types of peer support opportunities.

Volunteering. If you are interested, consider exploring volunteer opportunities with your local domestic violence agency or other nonprofit organizations that offer resources to survivors. Many survivors find meaning and purpose by volunteering, such as by answering hotline calls (again, with proper training in place), helping out at community awareness events, or collecting supplies needed by a local domestic violence agency.

Remember, paying it forward is entirely optional. Healing is a personal journey, and following your own path is important every step of the way. If giving back in this way doesn't resonate with you, it doesn't diminish your experiences or the impact you can have on the world.

Self-reflection questions for Commitment 6:

- *To what extent does the idea of "giving back" to others who have experienced abusive relationships resonate with you currently? Do you think this might be something that may be more or less appealing to you in the future? If so, why?*

- *If you do have an interest in focusing on giving back to others as part of your healing journey now or in the future, what types of giving back (e.g., volunteering, donating financial resources) are most and least appealing to you?*

Conclusion

In this chapter, we explored the broader context of overall healing from an abusive relationship and how financial recovery can be part of the healing journey. Each step you take toward rebuilding your financial stability and moving forward in your healing journey is a reflection of your strength and resilience. As you navigate this path, remember that financial recovery is not just about regaining control over your finances. It is also a journey toward reclaiming your sense of self and autonomy. As we've shared before, you can heal richer and stronger than you've ever been before.

Throughout this chapter, we reviewed the 6 Commitments in the Pathway for Supporting Survivors model (Murray, 2024). These 6 Commitments offer insights into integrating financial recovery into your healing process. These include the following:

- Being intentionally focused on your financial well-being and recovery (Commitment 1).

- Prioritizing any financial aspects of your emotional and physical safety needs (Commitment 2).

- Being patient with the potentially longer-term financial recovery process (Commitment 3).

- Taking deliberate steps forward toward your financial goals (Commitment 4).

- Practicing self-reflection to gain insights into your needs and experiences related to financial well-being (Commitment 5).

- Considering whether and how you may want to give back to others who have faced the repercussions of an abusive relationship (Commitment 6).

For many survivors, financial recovery is an essential part of their overall healing journeys. Each step along this journey helps you move toward a stronger, more empowered version of yourself. Healing from abuse involves more than just addressing immediate challenges; it's about creating a future in which you feel secure, valued, and in control.

As you move forward, be gentle with yourself and acknowledge your progress. Healing is a process, and each step is significant, no matter how small. Each step you take matters. Your journey toward financial recovery is a powerful aspect of reclaiming your life and building a future filled with hope and possibility. You have the strength and resilience to achieve your goals, and with each commitment you honor, you are creating a path toward a brighter, more empowered future.

Chapter 5
Committing to a Shame-free, Empowered Recovery Process

In Chapter 4, we explored the healing and recovery process following an abusive relationship, including implications for financial abuse recovery. Here in Chapter 5, we emphasize the importance of moving forward along the healing journey with a commitment to navigating this journey without shame and self-condemnation. We'll begin by exploring what shame is and how survivors of abuse may experience it both during and after an abusive relationship.

If only it were as simple as to say, "Shame, go away," and then all of our shame would immediately vanish! Unfortunately, shame can be deeply woven into our thoughts, emotions, and experiences. Therefore, we'll focus in this chapter on big-picture and practical approaches for understanding the potential influence of shame in your life, as well as how to move through and beyond shame along your healing journey. As you read this chapter, we invite you to reflect on the extent to which shame has impacted you and the steps you might take to commit to a shame-free recovery process moving forward.

Understanding Shame

The prominent shame researcher, Brené Brown (2013), defines shame as "the intensely painful feeling or experience of believing that we are flawed and therefore unworthy of love and belonging—something we've experienced, done, or failed to do makes us unworthy of connection" (paragraph 2). Unfortunately, shame is an all-too-familiar experience for many victims and survivors of abusive relationships. However, as we will discuss below, survivors can take proactive steps toward processing and releasing shame, both by addressing the existential dimensions of shame and taking practical steps to address it.

Earlier in this book, we mentioned the See the Triumph campaign and the related research that Christine and her colleagues conducted examining the stigma that survivors often face. Shame—from internal and external sources—can be a major contributor to that stigma. In the book, *Overcoming the Stigma of Intimate Partner Abuse,* Christine and her co-author, Allison Crowe, quote one survivor's experience with shame as follows:

> *It's difficult not to feel shame, which I'm trying to contextualize as a product of feeling some responsibility for the IPV (intimate partner violence). However, logically I know it's not a responsibility I should bear. I feel shame that I needed help—that I couldn't resolve it on my own, that I had to make use of the justice system. I feel shame that I spent so many years in the company of someone like my former partner. I feel shame that I'm not back on my feet financially, that I occasionally need help from my family.* (pp. 39-40)

This survivor's experiences illustrate how, even for survivors who recognize that they are not responsible for the abuse they experienced, shame still can rear its ugly head. This survivor's quote also shows how shame is often multi-layered. Shame can relate to the abuse itself, help-seeking, financial repercussions, and other associated experiences. Abusers also often contribute to survivors' shame through victim-blaming, disparaging words, and other power and control tactics.

In addition to shame related to the abuse, survivors also may feel shame about facing financial challenges. Many people feel shame around financial challenges, whether or not they have any experiences of abuse.

Because money is such a sensitive topic, and many of us didn't grow up learning much about financial literacy, we may find ourselves privately dealing with money-related challenges or hardships that feel embarrassing or shameful. Money-related shame can be exacerbated when we compare ourselves to others—or at least others' outward appearances—and think we are far behind where we "should" be financially.

In addition to shame connected to abuse and financial challenges, survivors may also feel shame regarding other aspects of their lives and experiences. This might include shame around being divorced, being a single parent, needing to work jobs that have a perceived lower status, not finishing a degree program, other painful life experiences, and decisions that didn't pan out the way we hoped they would. If it would be helpful to you, pause for a moment and reflect on the following question: *What, if any, aspects of your life and experiences bring up feelings of shame for you?*

Shame is a heavy feeling to carry around. Shame can chip away at our self-confidence and self-worth and hold us back from personal growth and healing. Shame also can be a difficult feeling to process and release. We can't necessarily just cast off all the shame we feel one time and expect it to be gone forever. Instead, working through and releasing shame is often an ongoing process throughout the journey of healing from an abusive relationship.

This chapter is about committing to a shame-free recovery process. However, we view a commitment to a shame-free recovery process more as an aspirational intention than a quick, easy, one-time decision. We encourage you to recognize when shame impacts you, find ways to process it that feel healthy to you, and actively challenge shame's grasp on your mind and emotions. Also, we invite you to focus on empowering yourself throughout your healing journey by actively reminding yourself that you can move toward releasing any shame that has unjustly been put upon you by others, including your abuser.

Throughout the rest of this chapter, we focus on approaches to addressing and moving beyond shame while recovering from past abuse. We'll start by exploring some of the more existential, big-picture aspects of addressing shame, and then we'll move on to more practical tools for processing and releasing shame.

Big-Picture Approaches for Addressing Shame

Looking back at Brené Brown's definition of shame that we presented earlier in this chapter, we can see how the experience of shame gives rise to many potential big-picture, existential questions for survivors:

- Am I flawed?

- Is there something wrong with me because I was involved in an abusive relationship?

- Am I worthy of being loved?

- Where do I belong?

- Who is responsible for the pain I feel? Is this my fault?

These questions are understandable responses to deeply troubling life experiences like abuse. Because isolation is such a common companion to abuse, it's even more likely for survivors to face these questions if they feel alone and different because of these experiences. After all, if we don't know many other people who also faced abuse, then we can begin to question our sense of worthiness and value, especially if we carry any level of self-blame for the abuse. Self-blame often results, at least in part, because abusers or others engaged in victim-blaming. It's natural to be more likely to feel shame about an experience that other people have directly blamed you for, even if you recognize that blaming you was wrong.

You might feel embarrassed if you grapple with big-picture questions like the ones listed above. These aren't the kinds of questions most people admit to having in day-to-day conversations with others. Just imagine if people were open about having questions and self-doubts like this! You might be in a work meeting, and someone would say, "I feel timid and insecure about speaking up about this idea I have because I'm afraid that other people will judge me." Or perhaps while chatting with your neighbor while walking your dog, they would say, "Wow, I've just been deeply questioning my overall self-worth lately."

There are many good reasons why we don't need or want to bare the deepest depths of our souls in everyday interactions with others as we go throughout our days. However, remember that just because people aren't openly talking about shame-based questions, this does not mean that they don't struggle with these questions internally. One of the unique opportunities that we have through our work as mental health professionals is that we get to engage in therapeutic conversations that often explore the realities of existential, shame-focused questions that clients are facing. Trust us when we tell you that it's often the people who *appear* to have their whole lives together who face some of the most profound experiences of shame.

We say all of this to normalize how common it is to experience shame-based thoughts and emotions, especially in the aftermath of an abusive relationship. As much as possible, resist the temptation to judge yourself as one of the only people in the world who experiences shame. Instead, remind yourself that you are one of many people in the world who experience feelings of shame. Be kind to yourself when you face shame-based feelings, and recognize them as natural responses to having faced unkind circumstances in life.

Recognizing that you are not alone in feeling shame is a powerful first step toward releasing some of shame's grasp on your life. Simply realizing you are not alone in feeling shame can help to reduce self-judgment and condemnation when shame arises. However, the big-picture processing of shame does not have to stop here. We can go further through deep reflection about the shame we feel to move toward putting shame in its rightful place. Christine offers these reflections on some of her experiences with shame:

Even today, years after my abusive relationship ended, feelings of shame about that experience creep in from time to time. However, shame is not nearly as big of an issue as it was in the early days of my healing journey. Back then, I often had such strong feelings of embarrassment for having been abused, for not paying attention to the warning signs or getting out of that relationship sooner, and for how much hurt I was carrying around because of the abuse. I would put much pressure on myself to "get over it" and "be strong" and move forward as quickly as possible.

Something that helped me was learning to actively challenge the thoughts in my mind that led to shame and embarrassment. When I would start to think, "I'm so embarrassed that I let him treat me like that," I would challenge that thought and replace it with, "He is the one who should be ashamed for how he treated me. The shame is his alone to bear." In truth, I suspected he wouldn't likely feel any shame given the long pattern of not taking accountability for his actions, but visually picturing the shame transferring from me to him, where it rightly belonged, was very empowering.

Christine's reflections highlight the potential value of proactively yet gently resisting shame when it rears its ugly head. We emphasize the word "gently" here because we know how important it is to be gentle with ourselves through all stages of the healing process. This isn't about creating a hostile battle in our minds. Instead, it's about caring for ourselves while proactively challenging the grip of shame on our minds and emotions.

Proactive, gentle resistance to shame will likely take some time and deep reflection. You can see that Christine mentioned that feelings of shame aren't wholly erased even today. Some survivors find it possible to move through shame relatively quickly, but if you need more time and effort, be patient while giving yourself grace and time. Shame can run deep within us, which is why we consider this process of proactive, gentle resistance to be an existential matter. Recognizing and reflecting on our experiences of shame may even help us to make meaning of our experiences, while also getting closer to the core of knowing and understanding ourselves.

We'll add one more big-picture consideration before moving on to more practical approaches for navigating shame. Through our personal and work experiences, we've seen the impacts of both internal (i.e., how we think and feel about shame) and external (i.e., how other people may treat us in stigmatizing and shameful ways) aspects of shame.

It's one thing to deal with our shame internally, and we may eventually gain inner peace from knowing we need not carry any shame about our experiences with abuse, finances, or any other aspects of our lives. And yet, even if we have made significant progress toward resolving the matter of shame internally, we still can face the external reality of judgment, mistreatment, and shaming from others. This might come from the abuser, as well as other people in our personal lives or professionals from whom we seek help. Because we can't control what other people think of us or how they treat us, this can become an area ripe for deep existential reflection. We can strive to acknowledge the hurt and pain their mistreatment causes while comforting ourselves in the face of shame-based messages from others.

Always remember: you are worthy of being treated with respect, but when people fall short of this, it does not mean anything is wrong with you. Other people's behavior is about them, and they bear full responsibility for their words and actions. This is not easy, but try to protect your healing process by frequently reminding yourself of your inherent worth. In addition to the existential issues discussed in this section, several practical tools and approaches can help us navigate feelings and experiences of shame when they arise.

Practical Approaches for Addressing Shame

Existential and practical approaches to navigating shame go hand in hand. Because shame can be so pervasive, it's wise to address it in as many helpful ways as possible. Practical tools are useful for addressing your immediate shame-related thoughts and feelings, while existential approaches help you dig deeper into exploring your underlying values and belief systems. You can gain valuable insights along your healing journey at both levels.

There are several helpful, practical strategies for navigating shame. We'll briefly review the following methods in this chapter: (1) processing your feelings, (2) practicing self-validation and self-compassion, (3) cultivating psychological safety, (4) gaining insight into your core beliefs and values, and (5) nurturing safe, supportive relationships. We address many similar strategies in other chapters of this book, but here, we focus on their applications to committing to a shame-free recovery process.

Processing your feelings. Many feelings can arise in relation to shame—such as sadness, guilt, regret, embarrassment, frustration, and anger. Allowing yourself to process your emotions fully is an important, yet often difficult, part of the healing process. Many survivors of abuse have developed ways to suppress or avoid their feelings as a protective mechanism, but learning to process your emotions can help you release the weight of shame. By identifying and acknowledging shame-related feelings, you can experience them without judgment. Recognizing your emotions—whether it's sadness, anger, or fear—creates space for understanding and processing them. It's important to remember that emotions, even intense ones, are temporary. Sitting with the discomfort and allowing yourself to feel your feelings in a self-supportive way offers opportunities for healing.

One approach to processing your feelings involves identifying and naming the emotions you experience throughout your day. Allow yourself to observe your feelings without rushing to fix or change anything. This can be as simple as asking yourself, "How am I feeling right now?" You might even consider setting reminders on your phone to check in with your feelings at certain points in the day. Journaling also can help externalize our emotions, helping them feel less overwhelming. Additionally, creative outlets like drawing or music can offer other forms of emotional expression when words are hard to find. Finding healthy ways to process our feelings promotes a shame-free recovery journey by reframing emotional experiences as a natural and acceptable part of healing from abuse, rather than something to suppress or hide.

Practicing self-validation and self-compassion. Healing from an abusive relationship is an act of immense bravery. Along the way, self-validation and self-compassion are powerful tools for restoring your self-worth and overcoming shame. Abuse often leaves survivors questioning their value and doubting their ability to make good decisions, which can lead to feelings of inadequacy or a fear of failure. By practicing self-validation, you acknowledge that your emotions, thoughts, and experiences are real and make sense. This simple yet powerful act can dismantle old, harmful narratives imposed by your abuser, thereby allowing you to reclaim your voice and affirm your journey. Self-compassion (Neff, n.d.) adds another layer of healing by encouraging you to treat yourself with the same kindness you would offer to a dear friend. This includes recognizing your humanity and that experiencing shame, fear, doubt, and setbacks does not make you flawed—it makes you human.

To practice self-validation and self-compassion, begin by incorporating self-soothing language into your inner dialogue. When shame or self-doubt arises, remind yourself that your feelings are valid and that it's normal to struggle. Phrases like "It makes sense that I feel this way" or "This is a feeling, and it will pass" can help ground you during times of anxiety and distress. Additionally, take a little time each day to reflect on your strengths and acknowledge your progress, no matter how small. This self-compassionate approach allows you to move through shame with grace and patience. For survivors, cultivating this self-compassionate mindset is especially important, as it shifts the focus from self-blame to self-empowerment. If it would be helpful, consider reaching out for support from a trained mental health professional for additional support in navigating shame by practicing self-validation and self-compassion. (See our book website at www.sourceforsurvivors.info/financialabuse for resources for connecting with support.)

Cultivating psychological safety. Cultivating psychological safety can help survivors rebuild self-trust and foster hope for a brighter future. Without a sense of safety, progress toward healing and financial well-being can feel out of reach. Psychological safety allows survivors to step out of survival mode, where constant fear and hypervigilance dominate, and begin to focus on their needs, goals, and aspirations. After experiencing an abusive relationship involving control, manipulation, and financial abuse, psychological safety is essential for reclaiming autonomy and regaining control over one's life.

Practical steps to restore a sense of psychological safety include using grounding exercises that help bring you into the present moment. When you feel overwhelmed or disoriented, grounding techniques like focusing on your breath, noticing the sensations around you, or engaging in mindfulness meditation can help anchor you. These practices help counteract the chaos of trauma, much like how a snow globe settles after being shaken. Therapy also can be a powerful tool for survivors, especially when working with a trauma-informed therapist who can guide you through coping mechanisms and address specific triggers. Additionally, incorporating gentle movements (e.g., walking or stretching) or using vagus nerve stimulation techniques like humming or gargling can regulate your nervous system and create a sense of physical and emotional calm. By restoring a sense of psychological safety, you can reconnect with your inner voice and feel empowered to take steps toward a shame-free recovery process.

Gaining insight into your core beliefs and values. Understanding your core beliefs can help you unlock clues to breaking free from fear- and shame-based thinking regarding the abuse you experienced or any financial challenges you're facing. Often, financial challenges are intertwined with deeply ingrained narratives from past experiences, including the abusive relationship itself. It's common to feel stuck in patterns of fear, shame, or unworthiness—emotions that can keep you from making empowered decisions regarding your financial well-being and overall healing journey. These old narratives, rooted in past trauma or unhealthy mindsets around money, often cause survivors to feel embarrassed, anxious, or fearful, which in turn limits their progress toward healing and financial well-being.

There is much value in the healing journey that comes with identifying and reframing any relevant limiting beliefs, especially regarding money and financial well-being. Reflecting on your history with money—whether shaped by your abusive relationship or other past experiences—can help you uncover unhealthy financial patterns and mindsets. Ask yourself: *How did my abuser control or manipulate my relationship with money? What stories about money have I carried with me, and how do they hold me back?* We'll dive deeper into this self-reflection in the next chapter, Chapter 6.

Remember that you can begin developing healthier ways of thinking about and acting with money so that you act from a place of empowerment, not shame. This might involve recognizing that you deserve financial security and freedom. Aligning your financial habits with your core values is key to achieving this shift. By doing so, you'll find that your financial decisions are not just about crunching numbers but about creating a life that supports a profound sense of purpose and fulfillment.

Nurturing safe, supportive relationships. Surrounding yourself with safe, supportive relationships is important for all aspects of the healing journey, especially when overcoming shame. Healthy relationships provide the emotional safety and encouragement needed to rebuild your life in a shame-free environment. Creating and maintaining clear boundaries with those around you is essential, ensuring that the people you allow into your life respect your emotional and physical limits. Supportive individuals nurture your growth, provide understanding without judgment, and help you feel safe as you work toward healing and financial recovery.

In your financial journey, it's valuable to connect with people who understand your financial goals and experiences, as well as those who provide support without judgment or condemnation, especially if your financial situation is not where you want it to be. Whether it's friends, family members, or financial mentors, these individuals can offer encouragement and practical advice without condemning or shaming you for past financial struggles. Be mindful of who you allow into your inner circle—focus on those who uplift you, respect your boundaries, and offer an environment where you feel empowered rather than shamed. By surrounding yourself with a community of supportive individuals, you can feel more secure and confident in your decisions, moving forward with the knowledge that you are not alone in your journey.

Conclusion

Hopefully, this chapter has offered you the opportunity to reflect on and normalize your emotions so you can process any feelings of shame in healthy ways. These practices create a foundation for moving past shame and fear and toward your vision of financial well-being and overall healing. Remember that healing from abuse and reclaiming your sense of worth is an ongoing process. The approaches we've discussed—from existential reflections to practical strategies—are valuable tools to help you rebuild your financial and emotional stability while also remaining committed to a shame-free recovery process.

The next chapter will dive deeper into the practical steps of taking stock of your financial well-being. By understanding your current financial starting point, you'll be better equipped to make informed decisions and set achievable goals that align with your values and long-term vision for your financial future. As you enter into this self-reflection, remember to proactively, yet gently, navigate through any feelings of shame that may arise.

Chapter 6
Taking Stock of Your Financial Well-being: Knowing Your Current Starting Point

As we move to this and the following chapters, please continue to remember the shame-free approach we discussed in Chapter 5. In Chapter 6, we'll offer tools to help you conduct a comprehensive review of your finances. This process requires self-compassion, courage, and an ongoing commitment to gentle resistance to shame, especially if you're facing financial challenges at the moment.

This chapter's financial self-assessment process is designed to help you gain awareness of how your finances have been affected by the abuse you experienced, along with an overall sense of your financial circumstances right now. It's essential to approach this process in a self-supporting manner because it can be challenging to take an honest look at our finances, especially if we've been hurt in this area by an abuser.

Financial self-awareness is valuable for several reasons. It's commonly said that knowledge is power, which is so true when it comes to managing our finances. People from all walks of life, whether they've experienced abuse or not, often avoid taking a deep look into their finances. Many people ignore stacks of bills and otherwise try to stay in denial over the realities of their financial circumstances. If you've been avoiding or denying anything related to money, know you're not alone.

Confronting negative aspects of our financial lives can be painful. However, ignoring or denying them doesn't make them disappear—and in fact, it can often make things worse, such as if that debt we've been ignoring continues to grow bigger as interest is added to the total balance.

At a practical level, financial challenges can significantly impact our ability to heal and move forward in our lives as survivors of abuse. At the same time, we can also identify areas where we're already doing well so that we can continue building on our strengths. Therefore, this chapter provides an opportunity for you to recognize what's going well, while also approaching with self-compassion any areas in which you may be struggling with your finances.

A comprehensive financial self-assessment is helpful because it allows you to identify your strengths, challenges, and areas that are relatively neutral or just okay. This assessment can help you better understand your strengths and growth areas, as well as the challenges and barriers you might face as you move forward on your healing journey.

Consider this financial self-assessment process an opportunity to examine the good, the bad, the ugly, and perhaps even the downright horrific aspects of your finances, always doing so with a healthy dose of self-kindness and patience. We invite you to approach this self-assessment with intention and curiosity. The information you gather throughout this process will provide a detailed understanding of your financial situation, laying the groundwork for the remaining chapters of this book. With this knowledge, you can more effectively identify priorities, goals, and action steps for rebuilding and strengthening your finances and other related areas of your life, such as your career pathway.

Also, this self-assessment can help you recognize areas where seeking outside guidance and support may be helpful. Whether it's from a financial professional, therapist, mentor, coach, trusted friend, or family member, having a clear understanding of your finances helps you to seek out the right kinds of help from potential supporters who are best equipped to provide it.

A Gentle Approach to Reviewing Your Financial Well-Being

Parts of this self-assessment may bring up discomfort or distress, especially if your abuser's actions impacted your finances. Gently approach this process. Our goal is to help you paint an accurate picture of your current financial situation so you can move forward in the best way for you within your unique circumstances.

As discussed in the last chapter, we encourage you to engage in this self-assessment without shame, judgment, or self-blame. If feelings of self-criticism arise, acknowledge them and aim to avoid self-condemnation. Consider the source of your feelings and thoughts, and seek alternative perspectives and information. Remember, this assessment is about understanding where you are now so you can make informed decisions about your financial future.

It can be beneficial to repeat positive affirmations or phrases to yourself when you notice negative self-talk coming to the surface. For instance, if you catch yourself saying, "This is such a horrible mess; I'm terrible with money," you could replace it with, "I haven't had enough opportunities to learn about my finances yet," "My financial well-being has been directly impacted by someone who was trying to hurt me," or "Understandably, things aren't where I wish they were right now. But with the right information and support, I can build a financial future that I'll feel great about."

Use positive self-talk, practice healthy coping strategies, and actively process feelings of judgment or blame by replacing them with compassion and kindness. Consider what supportive words you would offer to a best friend or loved one in a similar situation, and then remind yourself of those exact words (Neff, n.d.).

Other natural reactions you might experience are anger or being triggered when thinking about how your abuser hurt you. It's important not to pretend these feelings don't exist or rush through them. Instead, focus on processing them in healthy ways. Acknowledge when your abuser caused you harm, and know you did not deserve to be hurt in this way. Remember that you can take steps to overcome these hurts, but it's understandable to feel pain for what your abuser did and how their actions are impacting you today.

Find ways to process your emotions, such as writing in a journal or writing a letter to your abuser that you never send. Consider setting aside a specific time, perhaps earlier in the day, to address these feelings so they don't weigh on you before bedtime. Speaking with a trusted mental health professional or a close friend also can provide support during this time.

If you become highly triggered during parts of this self-assessment to the point where you want to avoid this topic and step away, know this is okay. This chapter and its process may require more space, time, and healing before you fully engage with it. Allow yourself to take the time you need. Remember that you're in the midst of your unique healing process, and there may be other areas in your healing journey that need more of your attention right now. You can always come back to the topic of finances when the timing is right for you.

This especially might be true if you're currently facing significant financial barriers or challenges, such as being embroiled in a costly custody case with your abuser or working multiple jobs to make ends meet. It's okay to prioritize what you must do right now and wait until you feel more prepared to take further steps to address your finances.

As you move through this chapter's self-assessment, maintain a sense of curiosity. You may even find the process enjoyable as you gain a deeper understanding of your finances and money-related mindsets and experiences. This chapter is comprehensive and uses a workbook-style approach that's somewhat different from previous chapters. You'll find plenty of spaces to write directly in the book. We recommend keeping a notebook handy to jot down your thoughts if you're reading electronically or need more space than the paperback version provides.

Given its depth, this chapter may take some time to complete. You might want to read through it first to familiarize yourself with the information before returning to fill in the details later. You might be ready to complete some parts immediately, while others may require time to gather information about bank accounts, debts, and other financial information. We suggest skimming through the chapter initially and considering what approach would be most beneficial for you. Then, proceed accordingly, engaging with the material in a way that feels right for you.

A Comprehensive Picture of Financial Well-Being to Guide Your Self-Assessment

As we begin this financial well-being self-assessment, let's revisit the definition of financial well-being from the Consumer Financial Protection Bureau (n.d., paragraph 2) that we reviewed in Chapter 1: "Financial well-being describes a condition wherein a person can fully meet current and ongoing financial obligations, feel secure in their financial future, and make choices that allow them to enjoy life. It's determined by the extent to which people feel that they: (1) Have control over day-to-day, month-to-month finances, (2) Have the capacity to absorb a financial shock, (3) Are on track to meet their financial goals, and (4) Have the financial freedom to make the choices that allow one to enjoy life."

In this chapter, we'll build on this definition by taking a comprehensive approach to looking at your financial well-being from many angles. This includes addressing practical aspects like your expenses and account balances, along with factors like your money mindset, skills, strengths, and financial memories. Let's begin with a few practical steps to help you prepare for this comprehensive review of your finances.

First, as we mentioned earlier, working through this chapter will require dedicated time and effort if you decide to work through it at a detailed level. However, all readers won't need or be ready for such an in-depth examination of their finances. You may have recently completed another financial self-assessment or received professional guidance already, or you may not be interested in diving deeply into your finances now. It's okay to honor your readiness and comfort level with this process.

For those prepared to take a deep dive, we encourage you to carve out time and space for this process. Committing to the process and actively engaging with the reflection questions and activities outlined in this chapter can help you understand your financial situation holistically. So, take a moment to assess your readiness to determine how much of a deep dive you're prepared to take right now, and proceed accordingly.

Think through how to create time for this self-assessment process. You may want to allocate a whole day or break it down into smaller, manageable chunks, such as 30 minutes a day for several days a week over the next few weeks. Choose a timeline that works best for your schedule and allows you to focus without feeling rushed.

Additionally, designate space for gathering and organizing the information you'll collect. Consider using a separate notebook or setting up an electronic folder on your computer to keep everything organized. Having a designated space to organize your financial information can help streamline the process and make it easier to track your progress.

In addition to these practical steps, it's important to have coping skills readily available to process any emotions that may arise during your self-assessment. As mentioned earlier, you may encounter complicated feelings or triggers related to your past experiences, so having coping strategies in place can help you navigate these emotions effectively.

If it is helpful, consider enlisting the support of someone you trust to assist you in this process. This could be a professional (e.g., a financial advisor or mental health professional) or a trusted loved one who can offer guidance and support. Eventually, you may even consider seeking out an accountability partner, which will be discussed further in Chapter 7.

As you move through the financial self-assessment, know that it's likely some topics will feel more difficult than others. Feel free to skip any sections that don't apply to you or that you're uncomfortable exploring right now. Remember, you're in control of your healing process and can empower yourself to make the right decisions for you at this time. Let's begin the financial assessment with this understanding in mind.

Your Comprehensive Financial Well-Being Self-Assessment

This assessment represents a present-day snapshot of your current financial situation. This is your starting point for today. Recognize that certain aspects might change if you were to revisit this assessment even a week or two later. To capture the timing of this self-assessment, begin by writing down today's date.

What is today's date? _______________________________

Section 1: Initial Reflections

First, take time to reflect on your motivation for doing this financial assessment, as well as for working to improve your financial situation more broadly. Identify your "why" for starting this process. Some examples might include building a more prosperous future, facing your financial fears, or affirming that you're worthy of building a solid financial foundation for your life. Finish the following sentences in the space below:

"I am doing this financial assessment because..."

"I want to work on improving my financial situation because..."

Next, identify coping and self-soothing skills you can use if and when intense emotions or memories arise while reviewing your finances. Here are some examples:

- Deep breathing exercises

- Mindfulness meditation

- Taking a walk or engaging in physical activity

- Writing in a journal

- Calling a 24/7 crisis hotline, like the 9-8-8 Lifeline (https://988lifeline.org/) or a hotline in your local community

- Talking to a trusted friend or therapist

- Listening to calming music or sounds

- Engaging in a creative activity, such as drawing or painting

- Practicing positive affirmations or self-compassion statements

Identify the coping strategies that resonate most with you (from the list above and any others that work for you) and write them below for reference if you experience distress at any point during your financial assessment process:

Next, we invite you to do some freeform writing to reflect on your overall thoughts, feelings, and actions regarding your finances. Set a timer for a designated timeline, perhaps five to twenty minutes, and write whatever comes up for you in the space below. Consider what's been happening in your finances over the past month, six months, or whatever time frame feels meaningful to you.

During this reflection time, avoid judging any thoughts that come to mind. Instead, allow yourself to freely write down any thoughts, emotions, or observations that arise without censoring yourself. This exercise can help you gain insight into your current mindset and attitudes toward your finances, serving as a valuable starting point for your financial assessment process.

My initial reflections on finances:

Section 2: Financial Literacy

Have you ever heard the saying, "You don't know what you don't know?" Often, we don't know what our blind spots are. But, informational blind spots can impact our ability to thrive in many areas of life, including our finances. A lack of awareness about financial matters can be risky because it can limit us from recognizing areas in which we might benefit from changing. However, it's natural and understandable to have limitations in our current knowledge, and we may not even know where to start or what we *could* learn to help us grow and progress toward our goals.

If you currently don't feel confident in your level of financial literacy (i.e., your knowledge about personal financial matters), keep in mind that many people are in the same spot. Financial literacy levels are relatively low across the general population—regardless of whether or not people have a history of abuse. According to the National Financial Educators Council (2023; n.d.), among over 70,000 people who have taken their 30-question financial literacy assessment, the average score was just 58%. This would be a failing grade in most traditional school settings! Moreover, the Council also found that people estimated that their lack of financial literacy cost them over $1,800 in the past year. Therefore, if your financial literacy levels are relatively low, know that many other people are in the same situation.

Evaluating your current levels of financial literacy can help you identify areas for future learning. If you're interested, we invite you to visit our website for this book, where you can find links to credible financial literacy quizzes and other financial education resources. You can see that site here: www.sourceforsurvivors.info/financialabuse

If you've taken one or more online financial literacy quizzes, jot down notes about what you learned from your results in the space below.

In addition to taking financial literacy quizzes, below are some additional reflection questions on your experiences with financial literacy and learning about money:

How, if at all, did you learn about money matters and personal finances? Consider your upbringing, family discussions about finances, personal experiences, and any formal education you received on financial matters.

Did you ever take a class in school to learn about money? If so, what do you remember learning? If not, what do you wish you would have learned while you were in school?

What is your current comfort level in reading and seeking financial information—such as through podcasts, articles, magazines, or books—to learn about personal finance? Rate your comfort level as high, medium, or low. Consider how confident you feel in understanding and navigating financial topics through various sources of information.

Section 3: The History of Your Relationship with Money

In this section, we explore your personal history around the emotional and family aspects of money and finances. Let's start by exploring some of your memories of money-related experiences.

Earliest Memory of Money: Write down your earliest memory about money. Describe how old you were and what happened in that memory.

Most Negative Memory of Money or Finances: Recall your most negative memory about money or finances. This could be something from your distant past or a more recent event.

Most Positive Memory of Money or Finances: Reflect on your most positive memory about money or finances. Again, this could be from your past or a recent experience.

Other Significant Money Memories: List any other significant money-related memories that stand out to you. These memories could be positive, negative, or neutral, but they left an impression on you regarding your financial experiences.

As you reflect on the significant money memories in your life, consider the impact of these circumstances on your current views and experiences with money by answering the following questions:

Impact on Current Views and Experiences: How do your past experiences with money influence your current perspectives about money and personal finances? Consider any patterns or recurring themes in your memories and how they shape your attitudes toward money today.

Physical Reactions: Reflect on the physical reactions as you explore money memories. Pay attention to how your body responds (e.g., with a stress response, calmly, headaches) when thinking about past financial situations.

Common Emotional Reactions: Think about the most common emotional reactions you've had over time regarding finances. Do you typically feel confident, stressed, anxious, or other emotions? Describe the most frequent emotional responses you have toward financial matters.

Messages Received About Money: Consider the messages you received about money and finances in your family while growing up. Reflect on whether these messages were positive, negative, or neutral and how they have influenced your beliefs and behaviors regarding money.

By reflecting on your money memories and how you think and feel about them, you can gain insights into the underlying beliefs and emotions that shape your relationship with money today. This awareness can help you identify areas for further personal growth and development.

Next, consider the community contexts of your upbringing, such as your neighborhood, faith community, and other relevant cultural and community groups. (Note: For these questions, please define "community" in whatever way makes sense to you, such as your neighborhood, a cultural community, or a spiritual/religious community.)

Internalized Messages: Reflect on the messages you internalized (i.e., adopted as your own beliefs) from experiences within the communities to which you belonged. Consider the cultural norms, values, and attitudes toward money that influenced you growing up. Did you observe any specific behaviors or beliefs regarding finances among community members?

Influences on Your Beliefs and Behaviors: How have your community experiences influenced your beliefs and behaviors around money? Consider whether the community-based messages you received aligned with those from your family or if there were discrepancies. Write below about how these influences shaped your financial mindset and habits.

Impacts on Financial Decision-Making: Assess the impact of your community contexts on your financial decision-making processes. Did you adopt or reject financial practices or attitudes based on community norms and values? Reflect on whether these influences have been positive or negative in guiding your financial choices.

By examining the messages internalized from your community contexts, you can better understand the external factors that shaped your relationship with money. This awareness can help you identify societal or cultural influences impacting your financial mindsets and behaviors.

Section 4: Exploring Your Strengths and Skill Sets

List of Your Strengths and Accomplishments: List the things you believe you do well in managing your finances. This could include budgeting, saving, investing, or any other areas where you feel confident. Don't be afraid to toot your own horn here! On the other hand, if you're struggling to identify strengths, consider asking a trusted friend or family member for their observations. We've started with a list of five items below, but feel free to add as many as you'd like!

1.

2.

3.

4.

5.

Rating Your Skills: Below, rate your skills level for each area from 0 (not at all skilled in this area currently) to 10 (highly skilled in this area currently). There's also a space to add other skills you want to highlight that we didn't include in the original list.

○ *Budgeting*: I am skilled at creating and sticking to a budget. _______

○ *Paying Bills on Time*: I consistently pay my bills by their due dates. _______

○ *Living Within Your Means*: I am able to spend less than I make and avoid overspending. _______ (Note: This one may be tricky if you are facing extremely limited financial resources now. In this case, you may find it necessary to spend more than you are making just to cover necessities like food and housing. Here, we encourage you to rate yourself more generally at keeping your expenses within your income, even if right now you don't find that possible.)

○ *Staying Organized*: I maintain organization within my financial documents and records. _______

○ *Meeting Deadlines*: I meet important financial deadlines, such as filing my taxes on time. _______

○ *Other Skill* (___________): _______

○ *Other Skill* (___________): _______

○ *Other Skill* (___________): _______

Financial Strategies and Systems: Consider whether you have any current strategies and systems to help you manage your finances. Examples might include setting aside weekly time for financial tasks or using specific budgeting tools or software. If you don't have any systems, acknowledge this without judgment and reflect on how it may impact your financial circumstances. In your own words below, write what (if any) systems you have in place currently related to managing your finances.

You can leverage the strengths and skill sets you identified in this section to improve your financial well-being moving forward. Additionally, assessing the systems you use (or lack thereof) can help you identify areas for improvement and develop strategies to enhance your money management practices.

Section 5: Emotional Spending Habits

Emotional spending involves purchasing decisions that are made in reaction to—and often to seek relief from—our current emotional states, and usually emotional spending refers to feelings perceived as unfavorable or distressing. Often, people who spend emotionally do so regardless of the purchase's long-term consequences or whether they can afford it. Examples of emotional spending include the following:

- Making impulsive purchases to feel better temporarily.

- Engaging in "retail therapy" to alleviate stress or sadness.

- Overspending during times of emotional distress without considering the long-term financial impacts.

Self-Assessment: Rate yourself on a scale from 0 (not at all) to 10 (very frequently) on how often you engage in emotional spending, and then write your reflections on how much you've used emotional spending patterns as a coping mechanism, as well as whether or how emotional spending patterns have led to financial troubles for you.

Coping Strategies Assessment: Below, write your thoughts on whether you currently use coping strategies that may inadvertently contribute to unhealthy spending habits or financial stress. For example, do you use mindless scrolling on your phone as a way to distract yourself in stressful situations, which sometimes leads you to make impulsive online shopping purchases?

Identify coping strategies that are currently working well for you in managing emotions that you could use if you'd like to avoid future emotional spending.

Consider alternative coping strategies to replace emotional spending, such as:

- Mindfulness practices to manage stress and emotions.

- Seeking support from friends, family, or a therapist during difficult times.

- Engaging in hobbies or activities that bring joy and fulfillment without spending (much or any) money.

- Developing healthy routines and habits for self-care, such as exercise, meditation, or journaling.

If emotional spending concerns you, write below what alternative coping strategies might be most helpful if you feel an urge to engage in emotional spending in a way that might be detrimental to you.

By assessing your emotional spending habits and exploring alternative coping strategies, you can work toward developing healthier ways to manage the impact of your emotions on your financial behaviors.

Section 6: A Deep Dive into the Numbers

Looking closely at our finances can help us better understand our current financial reality and how we want to move forward. Sometimes, facing the facts about our money can feel daunting, but it's an important part of our financial well-being and empowerment journey.

To guide you through examining your financial status, we've created the list below that includes suggested information to gather. By gathering these details, you will likely gain more clarity about your financial status and uncover areas where you can make meaningful changes. Remember, this isn't about judgment or criticism; it's about embracing your current reality compassionately and setting the stage for positive growth.

Take the time you need to gather as much of the information below that would be helpful to you. Feel free to skip any sections that don't apply to you.

Accounts and Balances:

Make a list of any and all current money-related accounts you have based on the following list:

- Checking and savings accounts: List all accounts and their current balances.
- Credit cards: Include all credit cards and their current balances.
- Other debts: Note mortgage, car loan, personal, and other debts, along with their balances.
- Other accounts: List any additional financial accounts and their current values/balances.

Net Worth Calculation:

You can build on the information you collected above in the Accounts and Balances section to examine your current net worth. First, list all your assets: Start by listing all your assets and the value of each one. Suggested assets are listed below, but there is also space provided to list other assets that are unique to you. You can leave blank any items that don't apply to you:

- Value of funds in any checking accounts
- Value of funds in any savings accounts
- Value of funds in any investments (e.g., stocks, bonds,

retirement accounts)
- Value of the equity in your primary home
- Value of the equity in any other investment properties
- Value of personal property (e.g., your car, jewelry, collectibles)
- Value of any other assets not listed above

Calculate the total value of your assets: Add up the values of all your assets to find the total. This represents the combined worth of everything you own.

Next, list all your liabilities: Next, list the amounts of your debts or liabilities. Again, we've suggested some potential debts below, but we've also provided space to add other liabilities that apply to your unique situation. Here again, leave any sections blank if they don't apply to you:

- The amount of credit card debt(s) you have
- The balance of your mortgage(s)
- The balance of your student loan(s)
- The balance of your car loan(s)
- The amount of any personal debt(s) you have (e.g., a loan from a family member or friend)
- The amount of any other debts not listed above

Calculate the total value of your liabilities: Add up the amounts owed for each liability to find the total. This represents the combined amount of all your debts/liabilities.

Finally, subtract your total liabilities from your total assets. Once you have the totals for both your assets and liabilities, subtract the total liabilities from the total assets. The result is your net worth.

$$\text{Net Worth} = \text{Total Assets} - \text{Total Liabilities}$$

As you look at the number above for your current net worth, what thoughts or feelings come to mind? Write your reflections in the space below.

Monthly Budget Numbers:

We will talk more about budgeting in Chapter 8. To help prepare for that discussion, in this section, you'll explore your monthly income and expenses.

- Income sources: List all sources of income, including alimony, child support, earned income, interest income, side hustles, and your primary job.
- Expenses: List all regular, occasional, and estimated monthly expenses, such as housing (e.g., rent or mortgages), food, debt payments, savings/investing, donations, taxes, etc.
- Note any financial support provided to family members or dependents.

Tax Information: Document tax-related details, including your last/current year's refund or payment amounts.

Missed Payments/Deadlines: Reflect on whether you missed any significant payments or deadlines recently and how this affected you financially.

Unique Financial Situations: Include any unique financial situations, such as inheritances, trust funds, alimony timelines, legal fees, possible legal settlements, etc. Make important notes regarding these unique situations.

Impacts of Abuse on Finances: List the areas of your finances that have been impacted by the abuse you experienced. Make notes below on how your experiences with abuse affected these areas.

Overall Reflections:

- Over the past year, would you say your financial situation has improved, remained the same, or worsened?

- Based on the information you gathered above, what are the areas of your finances that you feel best about?

- Also, based on the information you gathered above, what are the areas of your finances in which you feel most disappointed or overwhelmed?

- Just at a preliminary level, for now, jot down a few thoughts about your top priorities and financial goals. We'll explore this further in the next chapter, but for now, write your initial impressions below.

- Finally, if you want to capture additional reflections about this financial self-assessment process, write those in the space below.

Conclusion

If you completed this comprehensive financial self-assessment - Congratulations! You can feel proud of yourself for the work you did to complete this self-assessment. By doing an in-depth review of your financial situation, you've made an important move toward better understanding where you stand so you can map out your future financial pathways.

This self-assessment process offers a foundation for your future financial empowerment. It allows you to make informed decisions and take control of your financial future. Remember, this assessment is not about judgment or condemnation but growth and progress. You can use the insights gained from this self-assessment as a springboard for defining your next steps and setting achievable goals. This will be the focus of the next chapter, Chapter 7, which focuses on a process for financial dreaming, goal setting, and action planning. Whether it's paying off debt, increasing your savings, or investing for the future, you now have a sense of where you might focus your efforts. Keep this assessment on hand over the long term because it can remind you of your progress. Celebrate your achievements, no matter how small, and stay positive and motivated as you continue your journey toward financial well-being.

As you move forward, try to embrace the journey. Financial well-being is a lifelong pursuit, and while there may be challenges along the way, there are also many opportunities for growth and success. Trust in yourself, stay committed to your goals, and believe in the power of your resilience and determination. You've got this!

Chapter 7

Financial Dreaming, Goal Setting, and Action Planning: From Envisioning to Creating Your Prosperous Future

In the last chapter, we walked through a financial self-assessment process to help you gain a solid understanding of where things stand for you right now in the area of your finances. Now, it's time for what we hope will be one of this book's most enjoyable and empowering parts! Wherever you're starting from and however you feel about your financial situation today, in this chapter, we invite you to start dreaming about a vision for what a prosperous future looks like for you.

You'll also begin to think about how you can start to take steps - even small ones - to turn your dreams into goals, and then turn your goals into action plans that will bring those dreams and goals to life. This will lead us right into the following two chapters, which will further explore how to put your plans into action in your finances (Chapter 8) and career and educational pathways (Chapter 9).

As someone who has faced abuse, you may find it hard to dream of a brighter future for yourself. It's possible your abuser diminished your sense of self-worth and limited your sense of hope and possibilities for your life. We get that, and we've both been there as well. We've both also walked the path of rebuilding ourselves up to being able to believe again that we were worthy of dreaming of brighter days ahead. We know you can do this, too. We've not only lived this out in our own lives, but through our work, we've also seen countless survivors go from a sense of despair into building lives for themselves they never thought would be possible.

If you feel any fear or self-doubt about dreaming of a brighter future for yourself, honor those feelings, but try not to let them prevent you from dreaming and goal setting anyway. If at all possible, allow yourself to have fun with this process and even let yourself get a little (or a lot!) excited about it.

Some of the dreams and goals you have for yourself may feel far off, and many meaningful goals in life can indeed take a long time to realize. Some goals in life change or fall away, and often these are replaced with something unexpected that's even better than you could have imagined for yourself. Much of the joy in pursuing our dreams and goals is found in the *process* of working toward them, whether or not the end *outcome* is exactly what we expected.

As long as you're alive, time will pass regardless of whether or not you're intentionally moving toward your dreams and goals. It's up to you to decide how to use your time. Some people are genuinely content where they are, which is lovely if you're in this state of contentment right now! But if you have unrealized dreams about something you'd like to see in your life that isn't happening yet, then you can take steps today toward those dreams. Even simply acknowledging the dreams in our hearts is an essential step toward one day bringing those dreams to life.

For many years, Christine has been a graduate school professor who trains future counselors. Through her students, she's seen that people can start working toward new career goals at any age and stage of life. As a professor, Christine has had many conversations with prospective students about whether or not returning to school was a good idea, especially at mid-life or beyond. Her advice is always the same: the time will pass anyway, so think about whether you want to have that degree in a few years. There's no shame in deciding *not* to make significant changes like returning to school, as everyone has a unique path in life. However, don't let the myth that "it's too late to start something new" hold you back from pursuing the goals or dreams that lie deep inside your heart. Christine has seen students in their 40s, 50s, 60s, and even 70s begin their training to become counselors, and these students are shining examples that we can start new chapters at any time in our lives!

Because this is a book about financial empowerment following abuse, we encourage you to dream and create goals for your life that will impact your financial well-being, and this may include goals like returning to school or pursuing new career directions. But don't feel that you need to limit yourself to only setting goals in financial-related areas. The process we'll review in this chapter could be applied to just about any other area of your life in which you may like to see changes. Please take the information we'll cover and use it in any way that is helpful to you.

This chapter focuses on a continual process of dreaming, goal setting, and action-planning. Throughout this chapter, we'll cover each phase in detail, but remember that this process can be never-ending. You don't have to dream just one time and then never again! What often happens is that we see progress toward our dreams and goals through our actions, which leads us to dream even bigger and discover new goals that weren't on the horizon before.

Before diving in, we want to remind you to dream, set goals, and take action in ways that align with your vision for your life. Stay true to yourself in this process. One person may dream of speaking on a stage in front of thousands of people, while another may dream of helping people one-on-one. One person might dream of living in a mansion and driving a flashy car, whereas another person feels content with the dream of living in a small, simple apartment and using public transportation instead of dealing with the expenses of owning a car.

Each of us has unique values and visions for our lives. As you move through your dreaming, goal setting, and action-planning processes, keep checking in with yourself to make sure you're building the life *you* want. This will help ensure that you don't strive for goals based on others' expectations of you or comparisons you're making to other people's definitions of success.

Starting with Dreaming

Let's start with the dreaming phase, with a reminder that you can cycle back through this phase as many times as you'd like for the rest of your life. If dreaming feels uncomfortable - or maybe even impossible - for you right now, know that this is an understandable response for someone who has been in an abusive relationship.

Abusive and controlling partners can lead us to believe we don't have the freedom to direct our own lives. Your abuser may have systematically chipped away at your self-esteem. You may now feel like you don't even remember the dreams you had for yourself before the abusive relationship began. This is a heavy feeling, and it may take time to rebuild your capacity for dreaming again. If your abuser led you to believe you can't have dreams for yourself, remember that *this is a lie* and it's one you can overcome.

In this section, we'll walk through a series of exercises you can complete to begin dreaming for yourself and your future. These exercises are designed to help you explore the dreams you once had for yourself, including dreams that may have faded away or been diminished by your abuser. We'll also dive into new dreams that may start emerging for you, perhaps ones you've never considered. Try to stay open to a process of self-exploration and self-discovery throughout the dreaming process.

Exercise 1: Acknowledging lost dreams. First, let's acknowledge any of your past dreams that may have faded away, whether or not the fading away is related to your abusive relationship. Reflect on your earlier aspirations in life, whether from childhood or in your younger adult years. What did you envision for your family life, personal life, and career? Look for recurring themes, such as a desire to help others, even if your specific dreams change over time.

Now, consider any dreams you once held that were stifled or crushed by your abuser, either directly or indirectly. Did you have career goals or aspirations that they ridiculed? Did you have dreams you didn't dare express because you knew they would be dismissed? Use a metaphorical shovel to unearth these buried dreams, bringing them to the surface for examination and reflection. Remember, simply acknowledging these dreams doesn't mean you must pursue them, but they might offer valuable insights into your desires and aspirations for the future.

Exercise 2: Unrealized futures. In their book *Designing Your Life: How to Build a Well-Lived, Joyful Life,* authors Bill Burnett and Dave Evans (2016) introduced a fascinating concept by asking, "How many lifetimes' worth of living are there in you?" They claim that they've asked this question of many students they taught at Stanford, and the average answer is between three and four worthy potential lifetimes. They write, "If you accept this idea—that there are multiple great designs for your life, though you'll still only get to live one—it is rather liberating...There are many lives you could live happily and productively" (p. 67).

We agree with Burnett and Evans that it's freeing and empowering to embrace the fact that there are many potential pathways toward a happy, meaningful life. We can release ourselves from the pressure of figuring out just one "right" path for our lives. In this exercise, spend time imagining yourself living at least a few different lifestyles, from what you do for work and what your family life might look like to where you live and how you dress, eat, and spend your time. One sentence prompt that might help you generate ideas is, "I wonder what my life would be like if..."

As you envision what different possible versions of your life could look like, avoid the urge to feel you need to pick one pathway to follow now. Instead, focus on what clues you might discover within the visions you develop and what they tell you about the dreams hiding in your heart and mind.

Exercise 3: My dreams today. This exercise focuses on exploring new dreams emerging in your life today. Take a moment to imagine the possibilities within you, whether they're longstanding aspirations or newfound passions. Consider your dreams for your personal life, career, family, or any other areas of life. These dreams can be bold and ambitious or simple and heartfelt.

There's no need to judge or rationalize your dreams at this stage; allow yourself to dream freely. Take time to write down these dreams, giving each one space to unfold on paper. Don't worry if any of the dreams you write down seem to conflict with one another. Remember, this is an opportunity for self-discovery and exploration, so embrace the joy of dreaming without the pressure of immediate action.

We'll share an example here to illustrate the potential value in dreaming, whether or not those dreams ever become goals or action steps we take. This is a personal example from one of us, Christine, who has become a huge tea aficionado in recent years. We're talking about daily tea drinking, regularly hosting tea parties with friends, and starting a collection of teacups, saucers, and pots. Christine's love of tea has become such a part of her life that almost anyone who buys her a gift for any occasion (birthdays, holidays) knows to get her something tea-related! Christine wrote the following about how this love of tea is part of a possible future dream for her life:

I'm pretty obsessed with anything and everything related to tea! I have a fantasy dream of one day opening a tea house where I can share my love of tea with others. I can picture my dream vision of what the tea house looks like, and I even have a couple of possible names picked out! I love the idea of opening this tea house as a business one day, but honestly, I feel like I get as much joy from just having this fantasy as I might get from actually opening the tea house one day. I might even enjoy the fantasy more than the reality, as I'm sure running a tea house is not easy!

I've been asked whether this tea house is a fantasy or a goal I'll pursue someday. I proudly answered, "I don't know," when asked this question. For now, I'm comfortable not knowing if this will stay a fantasy or if it will happen. I enjoy my career working in the mental health and domestic violence fields so much, so I can envision being content with keeping the tea house a dream, but I also like having the idea in my mind to play around with. It also helps remind me that there are many different directions my future might take, and I hope to keep an open mind to see what happens.

Christine's tea house fantasy might seem silly to you—or maybe not! Either way, we hope it inspires you to explore even seemingly silly dreams in different areas of your life, including your work, family life, finances, health, and leisure time. We encourage you to take time to reflect on any dreams that are living in your heart right now. Allow yourself to explore and envision without feeling the pressure to make your dreams a reality overnight. Dreams are not mere destinations—they are journeys of self-discovery and fulfillment, waiting to unfold if and when their time comes.

Exercise 4: Dream Discovery Adventures. If you find yourself struggling to identify your dreams, especially in the aftermath of an abusive relationship, it's important to acknowledge that this is normal. Self-discovery and dreaming can be challenging if your self-worth and confidence have been affected by the hurtful words and actions of your abuser. If you're finding the process of dreaming difficult, consider setting out on some big or small adventures with a goal of self-discovery—a journey of exploration into your dreams and aspirations.

We're drawing inspiration from Julia Cameron's (2016) concept of the "Artist's Date," and we're adapting that concept into "Dream Discovery Adventures." It's a simple idea: set aside time to try new experiences and see what sparks your imagination. If you're stuck and unsure of your dreams, use these adventures to explore the possibilities!

You could watch a documentary related to a new potential field of interest or even interview someone already pursuing a passion similar to yours. For example, if you're like Christine and are passionate about tea, consider visiting a tea house and talking with the owner. Ask questions about their journey, passion, and the impact they hope to make through their tea house business. These experiences aren't about making commitments or decisions—they are about learning, exploring, and gaining insights into yourself and your potential dreams.

After each Dream Discovery Adventure, reflect or journal about your experiences. Write down what resonated with you, what surprised you, and any new insights you gained about your possible dreams. Whether you write notes on your phone or use a journal, the goal is to document your journey of self-discovery and ideas about possible dreams that spark your curiosity.

Exercise 5: Dreaming with Vision Boards. Vision boards can be powerful tools to support your dreaming process. A vision board offers a visual representation of your dreams, and vision boarding can help bring the ideas in your dreams to life.

There are many ways to do a vision board. A straightforward way is to get a piece of poster board (however big you'd like), some old magazines, scissors, and glue, cut out combinations of pictures and words that resonate with you, and then glue them on the board. If you want to get a little fancier, you can purchase vision board kits online, but the basic approach works well! Here are some vision board variations to consider:

1. *Whole Life Vision Board:* Create a vision board encompassing all areas of your life in which you have dreams or hopes. Include relationships, health, career, finances, friendships, and family. This comprehensive approach allows you to visualize your overarching life goals across different domains.

2. *Focus Area Vision Board:* Alternatively, you can build a vision board centered around a specific area of your life, such as your career, finances, mental health, or relationships. By honing in on one domain, you can dedicate more attention and detail to visualizing your dreams in that area.

3. *Time Frame-Based Vision Board:* Consider creating a vision board with a specific time frame in mind, such as a yearly vision board for the upcoming year that you create around New Year's Day. This approach allows you to set goals and aspirations for a defined period or stage of your life.

As best you can, visualize your dreams in vivid detail. Consider the emotions associated with achieving these dreams, envision how you want your life to look and feel, and be as creative as you'd like in representing those dreams on your vision board.

A few concluding reflections on dreaming. The process of dreaming doesn't have to be rushed or forced. If you find yourself needing time to articulate what your dreams might be, allow yourself to take the time you need. Give yourself time and space to explore and experiment with different possibilities. There's no rush; you can build your dreams with each step you take in this journey.

Throughout the dreaming process, keep checking in with yourself to ensure your dreams are your own. Listen to your intuition and identify what brings *you* peace and contentment. Also, let yourself dream without the pressure of commitment. View this as a brainstorming exercise—a space to explore the many possibilities that could lie ahead. Be mindful of the impact of any limiting beliefs or negative self-talk that may arise. Take note of these patterns and dare to challenge them, staying focused on building a future filled with possibilities, personal meaning, and fulfillment. Your dreams offer powerful clues into specific paths you might take in your life, and as these dreams crystallize, you can use them as guides for developing meaningful goals to pursue in your life.

From Dreaming to Goal Setting

Now, let's transition from dreaming to goal setting. As you've begun to envision exciting dreams for your finances and life, you'll likely start to recognize when the time comes to translate some of those dreams into tangible goals. However, as you navigate this process while healing from an abusive relationship, be sure to pace yourself and extend kindness to yourself along the way.

This section offers strategies for translating your dreams into actionable goals. Although we invite you to dream big and pursue big goals if that's right for you, we also encourage you to be okay with starting small. You might begin moving toward your goals with initial, tiny actions that you can use to build momentum toward your bigger dreams in the future. Remember, progress is made one step at a time, and every small step forward brings you closer to your ultimate vision of financial freedom, healing, and empowerment.

Through the dreaming exercises above, you might have identified anywhere from one to twenty or even more dreams you would like to pursue. We encourage you to keep a list of all those dreams and keep adding to that list over time! However, as you begin to translate dreams into goals, we suggest you focus on a small number (such as one or two) of dreams at a time. Pacing yourself is essential, especially if you're still facing challenges from the abuse and managing intense emotions and difficulties in different areas of your life.

Remember that any progress, no matter how small, is significant. Achieving small wins early on can build momentum for pursuing future goals. So, don't underestimate the power of starting with tiny steps. Setting and achieving even small goals (e.g., saving $10 this month) can start to build habits and increase your confidence and trust in your ability to set and achieve goals.

Consider the scale and scope of the goals you set for yourself and how many you might take on at once. Some readers might have the time and energy to pursue multiple goals at once, while others may juggle many responsibilities and face many challenges. Your circumstances and capacity will impact the pace of your progress, and that's perfectly okay whether you have hours to dedicate to your goal each week or just a few minutes a month. Honor where you are in your healing journey and continue to practice self-compassion and patience.

Focusing on what you can do, no matter how small, is important to making progress. Every action that is in alignment with your goals is a step in the right direction. Whether you wind up setting grandiose or modest goals, the process of setting and working toward goals is very similar. In the upcoming section, we'll share some valuable tools and skills for practical goal setting to help translate the dreams you identified earlier into actionable steps you can take toward creating them.

The goal setting process. Deciding to set a goal is an intentional first step toward achieving it. It's natural to feel overwhelmed by different aspects of our lives, whether related to our finances, career paths, or any big dreams we have. Yet, simply acknowledging our desire for change and committing to setting a goal is a big deal. Deciding to set a goal signifies a readiness to take steps toward creating a brighter future.

Let's start by introducing you to a framework for goal setting that you may have heard before: SMART goals. SMART is an acronym for Specific, Measurable, Achievable, Relevant, and Time-bound. You might have come across other versions of the words that make up the SMART goals acronym, but we'll stick to this version because it offers a lot of practical utility.

Setting a goal involves transforming the big ideas in a dream into a tangible, meaningful, and actionable target. This is where SMART goals come in. Below, we'll break down each component of SMART goals and see how they can help you turn your dreams into goals. Just for fun and to illustrate the SMART goals process, we'll apply it to Christine's example dream of opening a tea house one day to show the steps she might take to turn that dream into a goal if she ever decides to pursue it seriously.

- **Specific**: A goal should be clear and precise. When setting a goal, avoid vague statements and, instead, be specific by defining what you want to achieve. This often involves breaking down a big-picture dream or goal into specific steps to take along the way. For example, Christine's example of opening a tea house is a huge, long-term potential dream that would take a lot of time and steps to achieve. Christine might set an initial specific goal as a starting point: "I want to research and learn about the tea shop industry by meeting with at least five tea shop owners and visiting their tea houses."
- **Measurable**: A goal should be quantifiable so that you can

track your progress. Establish concrete criteria for measuring your success. For instance, in the tea shop example, Christine could measure her progress by tracking the number of tea shop owners she's met and visited.

- **Action-Oriented**: Goals should lead to actions you can take toward achieving them. Focus on what *you* can do more than on circumstances that are beyond your control. For instance, in the tea shop example, Christine's actions might include researching shop owners, sending invitations to schedule meetings with the owners or managers of the tea shops, and visiting tea houses.
- **Realistic**: Goals should be achievable, given your resources, skills, and circumstances. Set goals that stretch you but are within reach. Consider factors like time, money, and available support. For example, with Christine's goal of meeting and visiting at least five tea houses, Christine may identify some tea houses she would love to see, but if they're on the other side of the country or even the other side of the world, visiting them would be challenging! It'll likely be much more realistic to visit tea houses in town, or at least within a couple of hours of driving time.
- **Time-Bound**: Aim to set goals with a deadline or time frame for completion. Adding a timeline to your goal helps you stay focused. Set a realistic timeline for achieving your goal. In the tea shop example, Christine might set a deadline of three months to visit and learn from five tea houses.

Before we look at more examples and you take a turn applying the SMART goals framework to one or more of your own dreams, we want to add additional thoughts on goal setting in the context of the often long-term healing journey from past abuse. As we've discussed throughout this book, the abuse recovery process can be a long and difficult one. The reality for many survivors is that their finances, and possibly other areas of their lives, can look and feel like a total mess, which can be overwhelming and discouraging.

It's helpful to acknowledge your frustration and anger when goals take longer to achieve than you'd like, especially if you feel like you're in a mess because of the actions of your abuser. Honor your feelings, and practice self-compassion throughout the process. At the same time, know that you can be empowered to work toward your goals on a meaningful timeline that reflects the unique circumstances you're facing.

It may be helpful to think of your timelines in light of *accelerators* and *decelerators*. These are fancy words to describe factors that might speed up your timeline (accelerators) or slow you down (decelerators). You may have control over some of these, whereas others are factors that are out of your hands. For all people, whether or not they have a history of abuse, working through major financial troubles can take some time, and unfortunately, there are no quick magic tricks. We urge you to be cautious about your finances if anyone promises you quick fixes that sound too good to be true, as they probably are!

As you consider the timelines for your goals, start by thinking about your ideal timeline, and then ask yourself what sacrifices or compromises you want to and can make that might impact that timeline. For example, one person might theoretically be able to make more money to pay down debt quickly if they worked three jobs, but then they'd never have any time with their family, so that's not a sacrifice they're willing or able to make. On the other hand, another person might have fewer other commitments, so they might be willing to work a lot of extra hours to earn more money faster. These are personal decisions, so honor your needs, preferences, and circumstances as you map out the timelines for your goals that will work for you.

By applying the SMART goals criteria, you can create a clear and actionable plan for taking steps toward bringing your dreams to life. To further illustrate how the SMART goals approach applies to different types of dreams and goals, let's look at a few more examples:

Initial Dream: "I want to pay off all my debt."

- **Specific**: "I want to pay off $5,000 of credit card debt."

- **Measurable**: "I will track my progress by monitoring my monthly credit card statements and balances."

- **Action-oriented**: "I will allocate an extra $200 from my monthly budget toward debt repayment."

- **Realistic**: "Given my current income and expenses, paying off $5,000 of debt over the next 25 months is doable."

- **Time-Bound**: "I want to reach this goal within the next 25 months by making consistent monthly payments."

Initial Dream: "I want to build an emergency fund."

- **Specific**: "I want to save $3,000 in an emergency fund."

- **Measurable**: "I will track my savings progress by setting up automatic transfers of $250 from my paycheck into a designated savings account every month."

- **Action-Oriented**: "I will review my budget to identify areas where I can cut expenses and allocate the saved money towards my emergency fund."

- **Realistic**: "Based on my current income and expenses, saving $3,000 within the next 12 months is possible."

- **Time-Bound**: "I want to reach this goal within the next 12 months, ensuring I have a financial safety net by [specific date]."

Initial Dream: "I want to finish my college degree."

- **Specific**: "I want to finish my Associate's degree and then transfer to finish my Bachelor's degree at the public university in my city."

- **Measurable**: "I will meet with an advisor at the Community College to figure out how many credits to finish for my Associate's degree and to map out the plan for the courses I need to take to be on track to finish my Bachelor's degree in the subject I want to study."

- **Action-oriented**: "I will call the Community College Advising Office on Monday to schedule an appointment. I will ask the advisor I meet with to map out the steps I need to take to register for the classes I need and start in the next semester."

- **Realistic**: "Given the commitments I have at work and as a parent, as well as the number of credits I need for my degrees, I believe it is realistic for me to finish my Associate's degree in one year, and then I'll aim to finish my Bachelor's degree three years after that."

- **Time-Bound**: "I will do everything in my power (knowing that life can be unpredictable) to aim to graduate with my Bachelor's degree by the following date: ______________."

Now, try applying the SMART goals criteria to one of your dreams. Feel free to repeat the process with as many dreams as you'd like, but starting with one dream offers an opportunity to apply the process and build this skill. To hone in on a dream to practice with, consider the following questions:

- What is one dream you identified earlier that stands out to you as something you'd like to start moving toward as soon as possible?

- Once you've identified a dream to start with, what is one actionable step you could take to begin to move in the direction of that dream?

It's your turn now! In the spaces below, practice translating the dream you've identified into a SMART goal:

Write Down Your Initial Dream:

- How can you make your initial dream more specific?

- How can you make your initial dream more measurable?

- How can you make your initial dream more action-oriented?

- How can you make your initial dream more realistic?

- How can you make your initial dream more time-bound?

By applying the SMART goal framework, you can transform abstract or vague dreams into actionable goals that provide a roadmap toward bringing your dreams to life. This approach enables you to focus your efforts, track your progress, and stay motivated as you work toward achieving your goals in your finances and other areas of life. Once you've started to map out the goals you want to pursue, it's time to move from goal setting to action-planning, which we'll introduce in the next section and cover in much more detail in the following two chapters.

From Goal setting to Action-Planning

Now that we've covered dreaming and goal setting, it's time to move to the next phase of our process: action planning. Action planning already gets underway as part of the SMART goal development process, but we view action planning as taking further steps toward mapping out your next moves after you've mapped out your initial SMART goal. Specific to pursuing financial goals and educational and career goals, we'll dive a lot deeper into possible action steps in the following two chapters. However, in the rest of this chapter, we focus on an essential part of action planning: anticipating obstacles that may impede our progress and devising strategies to overcome them.

One common obstacle that can impact people's progress toward their goals is attempting to tackle too many actions at once. Often, we find ourselves overwhelmed if we're trying to pursue many goals at once or even a single, highly ambitious goal that we haven't effectively broken down into more manageable parts. Focusing on too many goals at once can lead to feeling overwhelmed and detracting from our sense of progress. This is particularly true when life is busy, and we juggle many responsibilities, commitments, and time constraints.

To counteract the temptation to attempt to do too much at once, consider prioritizing one manageable goal at a time. Breaking down significant goals into smaller, manageable steps can alleviate overwhelming feelings and enhance our sense of accomplishment. One example of a potentially overwhelming financial goal is starting to use a budget, especially if you've never formally budgeted before. Instead of starting with a goal of doing an overall budgeting process, you could start by exploring different budgeting apps or systems, testing them out, and then setting up the one that feels best for you. Focusing on one step at a time can gradually build your confidence and momentum toward achieving your goals.

Another obstacle to successful action is not having supportive systems in place. Systems help us set the stage for success as we strive to progress toward our goals. One effective system involves optimizing your environment by setting up small cues that make it as easy as possible for you to engage in your desired behaviors. For instance, if you have a fitness goal to exercise every morning, you might set out your workout clothes the night before or even sleep in them. Similarly, suppose you're working toward a financial goal of reducing your spending. In that case, you might put little signs in visible places in your house to remind you of this goal and consider setting up systems that make it more difficult for you to spend without planning. For example, you could remove shopping apps from your phone so you'd be required to go to a computer to make a purchase online. Without helpful systems, maintaining consistency in our efforts becomes significantly more challenging. Therefore, take time to identify actions you might take and devise systems or strategies to support your progress toward achieving your goals.

Another common barrier is forgetting to plan to replace undesirable behaviors with more desirable ones. Think through if there are specific behaviors you want to replace and develop a plan accordingly. For example, if you tend to spend money emotionally when you're upset, explore alternative actions for moments when you are facing intense emotions. Some helpful strategies include building your coping skills to process your feelings healthily or seeking support from a trusted loved one to avoid impulsive purchases. Additionally, you might focus on replacing the unwanted behavior with a positive alternative, such as practicing yoga or walking, to refocus your energy in a more positive direction.

Another possible barrier to taking action is a need for more knowledge. To overcome this obstacle, commit to ongoing learning as you move toward your goals. Fortunately, many free resources are available to increase your financial knowledge, as we'll discuss in the next chapter's section on financial literacy. However, be sure to assess the credibility of the sources you use. Remember, when it comes to finances, if something sounds too good to be true, it often is. Therefore, prioritize your commitment to ongoing learning and increasing your financial literacy as you make progress toward your goals.

Another barrier that can impede progress is the need for more resources and support. Tap into the resources available in your community and beyond to help set the stage for moving toward your goals. Resources may include websites offering credible information, nonprofit credit counseling services, pro bono legal assistance, counseling programs, and job training opportunities provided by women's or community resource centers. Community colleges often offer free or low-cost training programs and job skill development courses.

Another helpful strategy to build up the support around you is to seek out accountability partners. An accountability partner is someone you trust and feel comfortable sharing your goals with, particularly regarding your finances. Any potential accountability partners for financial-related goals should likely have a good bit of financial knowledge and skills and maintain a positive mindset to support you in your journey. Accountability partners are valuable because they provide external support and motivation. Having the support of someone you trust to encourage your progress toward your goals can significantly enhance your commitment.

Knowing you have someone to talk to who understands your goals can be a powerful motivator. If you don't have an accountability partner, consider seeking connections with people who might fulfill this role. Some people have one accountability partner, whereas others prefer to have more than one person serving in this role to seek out multiple perspectives when they have questions or need guidance. It could even be a professional, such as a counselor, who can assist you in managing emotional spending behaviors, for example.

Finally, another potential barrier is the belief that you should only celebrate goals when you completely reach them. While celebrating the achievement of finishing a goal is undoubtedly important, it's also valuable to celebrate the progress you make along the way. Take moments to acknowledge and appreciate your efforts, even small ones. Your celebrations don't have to be elaborate or costly; they can even simply involve taking a moment to experience a sense of gratitude for your progress. By celebrating your successes along the journey, you boost your confidence and reinforce your commitment to taking action.

Conclusion

Throughout this chapter, we've explored strategies to move through the processes of dreaming, goal setting, and action-planning. Remember, this is not a one-time process. Instead, it's a cycle you can repeat over and over again throughout your lifetime. As long as you're alive, you can continue to dream and consider which dreams you want to translate into goals that you start to pursue through intentional action. Of course, our dreams and goals will change over time throughout our lives, which is part of life's beauty.

Your experiences in an abusive relationship may have convinced you that you're not worthy of dreaming of a better life. We hope you've started to see that you *are* worthy of dreaming, healing, and building the most incredible future you can envision. If you have a hard time fully envisioning that now, hold onto the hope that the vision will likely become more clear as you continue your healing journey, especially as you build momentum toward your initial goals.

Practice patience as you make progress toward your dreams and goals. Remain open to your dreams and goals changing and evolving. Chances are, your life will bring unexpected twists and turns, and there might just be a lot more in store for you than you can even start to envision right now. Achieving meaningful change takes time, especially in areas like finances, where progress can sometimes seem slow. Take time to celebrate your progress in ways that resonate with you. As we move into the following two chapters, we will explore specific tools and strategies you can use to further your progress toward your financial goals in Chapter 8 and advance your career and education in Chapter 9. Remember, when working toward positive changes in your life, it's natural to experience moments of discouragement. Become your best cheerleader, seek out support from others, believe in your ability to learn and grow, and remain open to learning and seeking support where needed.

Chapter 8
Basic Financial Well-being Tools and Skills: Budgeting, Financial Literacy, and Self-Empowerment

In this chapter, we're shifting our focus from envisioning your goals to actively pursuing them in the area of your finances. After Chapter 7's focus on dreaming and setting goals, here in Chapter 8, we'll explore various tools and skills you can use to improve your financial well-being and start bringing your dreams and goals to life.

Coming up in Chapter 9, we'll focus on another important area that can shape your financial stability: your career and educational pathways. You can think of the current chapter as strategizing around managing the money you already have. Then, in Chapter 9, we'll explore how pursuing new career and educational goals might help increase your income, potentially providing you with more money to manage in the future!

Of course, increasing your income is only one of many possible reasons to explore new career and educational goals. However, if you find yourself frustrated while reading the current chapter because you've got limited financial resources available right now, then keep in mind that the career discussion is coming up soon. It's possible that exploring new educational or career pathways might open up future avenues for increasing your income and providing more resources to support your financial well-being.

This chapter will scratch the surface of several personal finance topics with basic information to enhance your financial literacy and confidence. Because each topic could warrant an entire book, we'll offer introductory overviews here to help you get started. Our goal is to alleviate the confusion and uncertainty you may feel about getting started addressing your financial situation, providing a starting point to empower you to take control of your finances. Our goal is to help demystify essential financial tools and equip you with foundational knowledge to help you navigate your financial journey with greater confidence and clarity. The tools we'll cover in this chapter are as follows:

1. Developing a Framework for Making Wise Financial Decisions
2. Building Your Financial Literacy
3. Setting Yourself Up with the Right Bank Accounts
4. Budgeting and Spending Planning
5. Dealing with Debt
6. Saving and Investing Strategies
7. Giving and Generosity

Everyone's financial journey is unique, and it's important to use the information presented in this chapter in a way that reflects your goals, needs, and current knowledge level. Consider this chapter as a starting point, offering information to help you start to build your financial well-being toolbox. If you find certain sections too basic or advanced, skip or skim through them accordingly. Our goal is to provide accessible guidance that can be adapted to your specific circumstances and objectives. Feel free to focus on the information that is most helpful to you at this point in time.

This chapter is not intended to be a comprehensive presentation of all the personal finance information or skills you'll need for the rest of your life. Our intention here is to provide a starting point, and for further exploration, we encourage you to visit our book website (www.sourceforsurvivors.info/financialabuse), where you'll find additional resources and tools to support your financial empowerment. The resources you'll find on the book website are designed to supplement the information provided in this chapter, offering opportunities for deeper learning and exploration of specific financial topics.

We'll add one other note before we dive into the first financial well-being tool about financial decision-making. Because we know many survivors are dealing with a lot of complexity in their lives, our core value when writing this chapter was *simplicity*. In our healing journeys, we've seen the importance of striving to keep things as simple as possible in the area of our finances while recovering from past abuse. There are a lot of complex (you might even say fancy) things that people can do with their finances. That's not the approach we've chosen to present here. We believe survivors benefit when they have access to simple, practical tools and information so they can set up their personal financial matters in a way that is as easy as possible to manage over time. At some point, you may find that you have an interest in exploring more complex financial arrangements. However, if you're just starting to rebuild your life and finances following an abusive relationship, then striving for simplicity can help set the stage for making consistent progress toward financial well-being and stability in your life.

Financial Well-Being Tool #1:

Developing a Framework for Making Wise Financial Decisions

With this first financial well-being tool, we encourage you to think about the big picture of financial decision-making. A guiding question you might consider is as follows: *What processes or safeguards do I want to put in place around making financial decisions to help me make the best possible decisions for me?* Three important considerations here include focusing on aligning your financial decisions with your values, building on positive support from others, and giving yourself the time and space you need to make important decisions. This approach can help you make decisions in a way that moves you toward the rich, fulfilling life you envision.

Aligning your decisions with your values. Engaging in values-based financial decision-making means considering your values and priorities in life when making big and small decisions that impact your finances. The more clarity you have about your values, priorities, and what's meaningful to you, the better you can use these to guide your decisions. Here's an exercise to help you clarify your values and connect them to your finances:

First, set aside some time to reflect on what is important to you in life and why. Write down these values on a sheet of paper. Examples of the types of values you might list include the following:

- Quality relationships with friends and family
- Spiritual growth and inner peace
- Maintaining a healthy mind and body
- Lifelong learning and pursuing meaningful career goals
- A calm, fulfilling lifestyle
- Adventurous travels
- Providing a solid financial foundation for your children, such as funding their education without significant student loan debt
- Living in a spacious home
- Driving a nice car (Note: With a value like this, it may help to further define what "nice" means to you, such as if you're referring to a specific price point for a car and/or a more general definition of "nice," such as having a reliable car that doesn't break down often.)

After you have your initial list, narrow it down to your top three to five values. You can circle or star these to emphasize their importance to you. Consider what truly matters most as you narrow down to a few fundamental values. Once you have identified your top values, reflect on how they translate into financial decisions. For instance:

- If quality time with family and friends is your top value, you may prioritize budgeting for experiences like vacations or gatherings over material possessions.
- If living in a cozy, well-kept home is important to you, you might allocate funds for home maintenance and improvements rather than spending on extravagant vacations.
- Spiritual growth could include budgeting for a spiritual retreat or meditation classes.
- Investing in your health might mean allocating funds for gym memberships or healthy food choices.
- Pursuing career goals might involve budgeting for professional development courses or saving for a career transition.

Next, identify potential conflicts or tensions among your financial values and develop strategies for how to navigate them. Being clear about your values helps you make decisions that align with what matters most to you, even as your values and priorities may shift over time. This clarity guides your financial decisions and allows you to stay true to your core values when faced with new choices.

By aligning your financial decisions with your values, you create a personal roadmap that can lead to economic well-being, while also honoring what matters most to you. Remember that your priorities may change over time, so make time to reflect regularly on how your current values might impact your financial decision-making.

Seeking guidance and support from others. Seeking support and accountability can be extremely helpful when making financial decisions, but seeking support from the wrong sources can potentially derail you. It's important to choose wisely when it comes to who you'll rely on for guidance and moral support when you're making financial decisions.

Consider having an accountability partner who can provide guidance and support along your financial journey. This could be a professional financial adviser or someone close to you, such as a friend, partner, or family member you trust with the details of your financial life. Having someone to turn to for advice when facing major financial decisions can be very reassuring.

Be mindful of the financial advice that you seek and receive. While seeking advice and guidance can be helpful, be selective about the sources of financial information you rely on. Consider the credibility, expertise, and motivations of the advisors or voices you listen to, ensuring their recommendations align with your goals and values. By leveraging your support networks, consulting reputable professionals, and staying informed about financial resources, you can make more informed and effective financial decisions that contribute to your long-term financial well-being.

Giving yourself time to make financial decisions. When making significant financial decisions, take the time you need to make the best choices for yourself. Financial decisions sometimes come with pressure or a sense of urgency, especially when you're faced with a situation like the rent being due when you don't have any money in the bank. Although you may face instances in which you face real deadlines, give yourself time and space before making significant decisions whenever possible. This allows you to consider all factors and make a decision that aligns with your current circumstances and long-term goals.

If you find yourself under stress or feeling pressured, or if old money habits and mindsets resurface, take a moment to acknowledge these feelings and thoughts. Examine decisions from both a logical perspective and by tuning into your emotions. Being mindful of how your emotions may influence your decisions can help you avoid making reactive choices that may not be in your best interest in the long run. Taking time to assess your options and understand your feelings can lead to more informed and beneficial financial decisions.

Financial Well-Being Tool #2:

Building Your Financial Literacy

The second financial well-being tool is a cornerstone of financial empowerment: financial literacy. While we've touched on this topic in previous chapters, we're revisiting it here for a deeper dive. As we discussed earlier, many people—whether or not they are survivors of abusive relationships—have pretty low levels of financial literacy, so there's no need for judgment or shame if your financial literacy starting point is relatively low.

If you're already familiar with some basics, then more advanced financial knowledge can help you continue to understand and manage your finances more effectively over time. Regardless of where you're starting from, financial literacy is a knowledge base that can be developed and strengthened. An ongoing commitment to building your financial literacy can equip you with valuable knowledge to navigate your financial journeys with greater confidence and clarity.

To enhance your financial literacy, consider what types of learning are most appealing and accessible in this season of your life. What types of learning seem most fun and exciting and most easily integrated into your schedule? Examples might include enrolling in online or in-person classes offered by organizations like women's resource centers, community colleges, faith communities, or nonprofit credit counseling agencies in your area. Additionally, you can explore online financial literacy courses available through online platforms, examples of which you can access via our book website (www.sourceforsurvivors.info/financialabuse).

However, while taking formal classes can be helpful, it's not the best fit for everyone. Explore other options for boosting your financial literacy. For instance, you could read books dedicated to financial literacy, even if you can only commit to reading a few pages a week. You could also check out podcasts and TV shows that cover financial topics, tapping into the many resources available in today's digital landscape. Financial podcasts can be a great way to expand your financial literacy while commuting, exercising, or doing household chores. As we've emphasized throughout this book, look into the credibility of any resources you choose to ensure you receive accurate and reliable information.

There are also many valuable online resources available to help people increase their financial literacy. You can start by visiting reputable websites with helpful articles or tutorials on financial topics. Additionally, consider following financial educators on social media platforms for regular insights and tips. By subscribing to newsletters or joining online communities focusing on financial education, you can make it as easy as possible to stay updated on the latest trends and information. These steps provide convenient ways to incorporate ongoing learning into your daily routine.

Again, be very discerning about the credibility of any financial literacy resources you're considering. A helpful question to ask yourself is whether the information provided genuinely aims to help people or if it is primarily focused on selling a product or service. Fee-based products or services aren't necessarily bad. Still, many credible and free resources exist to begin your financial education journey, and you don't necessarily need to spend money to learn more about money management.

Why is it so important to be cautious about the credibility of financial information? Unfortunately, some individuals and organizations in the financial space will prioritize their profit over your best interests. Look for sources emphasizing sound economic principles rather than promising unrealistic gains or quick fixes. It is wise to have a healthy dose of skepticism while checking out new financial literacy resources. This is especially true as a survivor of abuse, as your vulnerable circumstances and feelings about your finances right now may make you a prime target for an exploitative scammer. If you're just starting with your financial abuse recovery process, focus on clearly credible resources as you're building your knowledge base.

Financial Well-Being Tool #3:

Setting Yourself Up with the Right Bank Accounts

Opening a bank account might seem like an overly basic financial topic. However, it's not uncommon for survivors of abusive relationships to have had limited or no access to any financial accounts due to their abusers' control. Even if you already have access to your own accounts, you may still feel confused or overwhelmed about the number and types of accounts you have or would want to manage your finances in a way that feels right to you.

We suggest a simplified, streamlined approach involving a reasonable number of bank accounts, each of which serves a purpose in managing your finances. For some survivors, a single checking account may be all that is needed, whereas others may require multiple accounts. Consider your unique circumstances as you read further to decide what arrangements might work best for you. Reviewing the different types of bank accounts is a helpful starting point.

A *savings account* is useful for holding money you won't need immediate access to. Savings accounts may offer slightly (and we really mean slightly!) higher interest rates than checking accounts. Savings accounts may not provide as easy access to your funds as a checking account, such as by not being associated with a debit card or checks. Some savings accounts are considered *high-yield* or *high-interest* because they offer higher-than-usual interest rates than more standard savings accounts.

If you're unfamiliar with interest, it is essentially the percentage of money earned on the balance of your funds in an account. So, if you have $10,000 in an account that earns 1% in interest annually, the interest earned during the year will be $100 ($10,000 * 1% = $100). The interest you *earn*, such as from savings accounts or investments, adds to your financial assets. On the other hand, interest that you *owe*, such as interest you're charged on a credit card or car loan, subtracts from your financial assets. Paying more attention to interest rates on your assets and debts is a great way to increase your financial literacy if you're not already paying attention to them!

A *checking account* is useful for managing day-to-day transactions, such as receiving your paycheck and paying bills. Checking accounts typically offer many options for spending funds, including a debit card, paper and online checks, and access to online money transfer services (e.g., PayPal or Zelle).

There are other types of bank accounts to consider as well. These include the following:

- *Money market accounts* combine some features of savings and checking accounts and have slightly higher interest rates than traditional savings accounts.

- *Certificates of Deposit (CDs)* are accounts in which you commit to keeping your funds in the account locked in for a designated time frame (e.g., 6 months, a year, or multiple years) in exchange for a somewhat higher interest rate.

- *Investment accounts*, including retirement accounts, taxable investment accounts, Individual Retirement Accounts (IRAs), and educational investment accounts (e.g., 529s). We'll talk more about investing later in this chapter!

Understanding the differences between types of accounts can help you make informed decisions about where to put your funds based on your financial goals and needs.

In deciding what types of accounts to open, you'll also want to think through which bank(s) to work with. Seek out information about different banks to compare their rates and services. You might prefer a large national bank that has a physical branch location in your area, a fully online bank, or a smaller local or regional bank. Consider your preferences regarding in-person banking services versus online banking. Some people like meeting with a bank representative in person, while others prefer the convenience of online banking.

Explore the tools and resources offered by different banks, including online banking features and perks, to enhance your financial management experience. All options have advantages and drawbacks, so choose what would work best for you based on your needs and preferences. Look into how each bank handles any fees associated with their accounts, such as monthly maintenance fees or overdraft charges.

Also, think through how many banks you want to work with and how many accounts you want to have overall. Consolidating your accounts within a single bank can simplify your finances, but having accounts at multiple banks may be beneficial for diversification or if you have a large number of assets. Ultimately, select banking options that best suit your personal goals and circumstances.

Prioritize the security and privacy of your accounts, particularly if you have concerns about potential interference from your past abuser(s). Talk with bank representatives to understand your account's security features and privacy settings. Use caution when setting passwords, and avoid using any that a former partner might easily guess. Taking these precautions helps to safeguard your financial information when managing your finances in the aftermath of an abusive relationship.

Overall, try to set up your bank accounts to maximize your peace of mind and provide you with as much ease in managing your accounts as possible. Aim for a comfortable and manageable setup, especially considering your journey as a survivor. Simplifying your finances can reduce unnecessary stress and complexity while navigating other aspects of your healing journey.

Financial Well-Being Tool #4:

Budgeting and Spending Planning

Budgeting and spending planning are valuable tools to support your financial well-being. While the idea of budgeting may seem daunting or restrictive, remember that budgeting (or some variation of it that makes sense to you) can be a practical tool for gaining control over your finances. If you don't already have a personal budget, you can start by referencing the information you gathered through the self-assessment in Chapter 6, where you reviewed your monthly expenses and income.

This assessment offers a foundation for creating a budget or spending plan tailored to your financial circumstances.

Many budgeting tools are available, each offering unique features and benefits. Exploring different budgeting tools and apps can be an interesting—and perhaps even fun—part of managing your finances. (Although we're sure some of you think we're going too far by calling anything budget-related fun!) Your options range anywhere from writing out your budget on a spreadsheet or document to using some of the newer technology-based budgeting apps and websites that are available.

In addition to providing a sample downloadable budgeting Excel file at our book's website (www.sourceforsurvivors.info/financialabuse), we encourage you to explore the diverse range of budgeting tools and apps available today. This includes several easily accessible apps and budgeting tools, although some do charge fees that you'll want to factor into your decisions. You can go as high- or low-tech as you'd like when it comes to budgeting, and there's nothing wrong with a low-tech, accessible approach to budgeting if that's your style! For instance, Christine has developed and refined her budgeting spreadsheet in Excel over nearly two decades, finding it to be the most effective tool for her needs. Even as new budgeting apps have become available, she's opted to stick with her trusted, simple spreadsheet due to its familiarity and how much she has customized it to her needs over time.

Budgeting apps can be handy if you're managing your finances with others, whether it's older children or a new partner with whom you're creating a household budget. Budgeting apps often have features to facilitate collaboration and sharing, making it easier to coordinate financial planning and track expenses collectively. If you'll be sharing your budgeting process with anyone else, exploring the collaborative features of budgeting apps could streamline your financial management processes.

Balancing your income and expenses is a first step in the budgeting process. Whenever possible, it's wise to live within your means, meaning that the money you bring each month is more than what you spend. This may not always be possible, especially when recovering from an abusive relationship. If you cannot do this, consider how you might start working toward this goal over time.

It's useful to set specific time frames for your budgeting processes. Many people work with a monthly budget, which can make sense because many regular bills (e.g., rent and utilities) occur on a monthly basis. However, there's no requirement to use a monthly budget timeline, and you may find a shorter (e.g., biweekly if that's your timeline for getting paychecks) or longer (e.g., quarterly if you own a small business that runs on a quarterly financial schedule). In general, however, be cautious about using too long of a budgeting timeframe. For example, trying to budget for a whole year would likely get pretty overwhelming.

To start setting up your budget, list all of your sources of income during the designated budgeting time frame, including your work earnings and any other sources like child support. Then, list your essential expenses for that same time frame, such as housing, food, transportation, and educational expenses for children. By allocating your income to cover your necessities first, you can focus on stability in your financial planning.

Once you've covered your essential expenses, you can allocate any remaining funds toward your other interests (e.g., entertainment, gifts, and hobbies), as well as your bigger financial goals, such as by paying down debt or saving for an upcoming expense. By incorporating your goals into your budgeting process, you can align your financial decisions with your long-term objectives.

Setting up your budget is an important first step. Next, it's important to plan on tracking your expenses in line with your budget. Tracking your expenses based on your budget categories helps maintain a sense of control over your finances. It's understandable if tracking your expenses feels tedious, especially in the midst of a busy life. However, tracking your expenses allows you to monitor your spending habits and stay within your budget. Budgeting apps or tools your bank provides can streamline this process and make it more manageable.

Staying aware of your expenses helps you make informed decisions about adjustments you may need to make to your budget. Over time, you may notice differences between your budgeted amounts and actual spending. For instance, if you consistently spend $800 per month on groceries for your family instead of your budgeted amount of $500, you'll likely need to adjust your budget accordingly, at least if you can't cut your expenses further. This might involve reallocating funds from other categories, such as discretionary spending, to cover increased grocery expenses.

Think of your budget as a living document. You'll want to change it as you learn more and adjust your spending patterns, as well as to reflect your changing goals over time. For example, once you pay off a debt that you've had in your budget, you can reallocate those funds to another expense or category. Budgeting isn't a one-time task. Instead, it's an ongoing process for managing, tracking, and adjusting your spending and saving over time.

By regularly reviewing and adjusting your budget, you can see whether it accurately reflects your financial priorities and goals. Budgeting can be a helpful, practical tool for taking control of your finances and working toward your goals as a survivor of an abusive relationship.

While budgeting may seem overwhelming or boring initially, the insights gained from tracking your expenses and adjusting your budget can be very helpful in gaining a sense of control over your finances.

Remember, a budget is not meant to restrict you but rather to empower you to make informed decisions about how you use your money. By proactively managing your finances through budgeting, you can build a solid foundation for achieving your financial goals and navigating challenges that arise along the way.

Financial Well-Being Tool #5:

Dealing with Debt

In this section, we'll explore strategies for managing debt, which is a challenge faced by many people, whether or not they have a history of an abusive relationship. Dealing with debt is a common aspect of financial life, although there are some nuanced debt-related challenges that survivors may face.

Some readers might currently be debt-free, which is fantastic because being debt-free can offer you greater freedom and flexibility, especially as you're healing from the past and pursuing your financial goals. However, many survivors find themselves burdened with debt when leaving an abusive relationship.

This section aims to provide information to help you assess your existing debts, make informed decisions about potential future debts, and develop a mindset and strategy around debt management. This way, you can align your debt decisions with your values and effectively navigate debt while pursuing other goals and dreams.

We want to begin by addressing a painful reality that some survivors face: the debt they carry may be a result of their abuser's actions. As we discussed in Chapter 3, this could involve the abuser taking on debt in the survivor's name, committing fraud, or making decisions about debt without considering the survivor's perspective or values. Debt also might be the result of expensive legal costs accrued during drawn-out divorce or custody cases in court. If you find yourself in any of these situations dealing with unjust or unfair debt, we acknowledge how painful this can be. It's important to remember that this situation is not your fault, and you are not to blame for the harmful actions of your abuser.

If you have any suspicion that your abuser engaged in illegal or fraudulent activities that resulted in debt in your name without your consent, such as opening credit cards or loans using your personal information, consider consulting with a lawyer or law enforcement. They can help determine if there are legal actions you can take to address the situation to hold your abuser accountable for their actions. Safety considerations should always be a priority as you explore these options. We also recommend working with a victim advocate and developing a safety plan if you decide to pursue legal recourse and have concerns about potential retaliation from your abuser. If you suspect your abuser committed fraud or identity theft, take time to explore your options, seek information and support, and evaluate whether pursuing legal action could benefit your situation.

Regardless of whether your abuser directly inflicted damage in the area of your debts, we encourage you to take your credit records seriously, especially if your abuser had or continues to have access to your personal information, such as your Social Security Number and other personal records. A recommended first step is to obtain a credit report from each of the three major credit reporting agencies: Equifax, Experian, and TransUnion. Every consumer in the U.S. is entitled to one free credit report per year, which you can learn more about by visiting our book website (www.sourceforsurvivors.info/financialabuse).

Pulling your credit history and credit score serves several important purposes. First, it helps you to gain a comprehensive and accurate understanding of your credit records, including positive, negative, or neutral aspects. Reviewing your credit history also lets you see a snapshot of all your current debts. Additionally, monitoring your credit report and score can help you detect any unauthorized attempts by your abuser (or anyone else) to open accounts or incur debts in your name.

Subscribing to a credit monitoring service can be valuable, although these services usually have fees. While not everyone may choose this option, we recommend, at minimum, pulling your credit report now and then, as well as setting a reminder to do so at least annually moving forward. This regular check-in is so valuable, especially if you're concerned your abuser may try to exploit your information for fraudulent purposes or identity theft.

Once you've pulled your credit report, review it closely to gain a complete picture of all your current and closed debts. Also, reviewing your credit report allows you to identify factors influencing your credit score, which can offer helpful insights into areas needing improvement or attention.

To effectively manage debts, a helpful starting point is to create a detailed list that includes all your debts, their types, balances, and interest rates. You may have already done this as part of the financial self-assessment covered in Chapter 6. Here's a breakdown of the information you can include in your debt list if you haven't already gathered this information:

- *Type of Debt*: Specify the type of each debt, such as student loans, car loans, home loans, personal loans, credit cards, or store cards.

- *Balance*: Record each debt's outstanding balance. You can find this information by checking your most recent statements or logging into your accounts.

- *Interest Rate*: Note down the interest rate associated with each debt. This information will help you prioritize debts and develop a repayment strategy.

It's natural to feel overwhelmed if you have a lot of debt right now. Although it may take time to work through these debts, it can help to start by developing plans and systems to begin moving toward paying down or off your debts, especially if that's an important goal for you.

Communication with creditors is helpful if you're experiencing financial hardships that might make it hard to pay down debt if you're struggling to make ends meet. Reach out to ask about hardship programs, like pausing repayments or adjusting payoff plans, and also be mindful of their policies around whether and how much interest will continue to accrue even if they allow you to pause payments for some time.

If you need individualized guidance and support for managing your debts, seek out credible sources of support, such as financial counseling or debt consolidation services. Again, we can't emphasize enough how important it is to be cautious about only using credible and trustworthy resources. Look for organizations that have a proven track record of helping clients manage debt effectively, such as local nonprofits affiliated with the National Foundation for Credit Counseling (https://www.nfcc.org/). Keep in mind that there are some "bad seeds" out there in terms of people and organizations that exploit people who are in vulnerable situations with debts.

When seeking professional advice about your debts, consider bringing a trusted friend or family member along to meetings for added support and guidance. Having someone else present can help address any questions or concerns that may arise and help you make informed decisions about managing your debt effectively.

If you're in really dire straits and have reached a point of considering bankruptcy, seek guidance from reputable professionals, including a credible, knowledgeable attorney in your community. Bankruptcy is a significant decision with long-term consequences, such as impacting your credit score, future credit options, housing applications, and job prospects. To help you make decisions about a possible bankruptcy filing, learn about the various types of bankruptcy, their implications, and whether they involve debt elimination or repayment. Gather as much information as possible and carefully weigh your options before making any final decisions. Managing high levels of debt can be incredibly stressful, so prioritize taking good care of yourself and seeking the support you need to navigate this challenging situation wisely.

Another common debt-related concern is having a low credit score. Your credit score can impact your life in many ways, especially when rebuilding your life after an abusive relationship and other financial challenges. A low credit score could affect your ability to obtain credit, secure housing, or even land a job. While this book doesn't have room to extensively cover strategies for improving your credit score, we've provided links for more information on this topic on our book's website. Improving your credit score may take time, but you can begin taking steps toward that goal, even if the steps you can take seem small right now.

If you're concerned about identity theft or fraud—especially if you think your abuser might try to do this to you—then placing a freeze on your credit could provide you with added security. However, remember that unfreezing your reports may be necessary when applying for loans or other credit-related needs, so this could add some level of time and hassle for you. Taking the step of freezing your credit could be a wise step, but be sure to educate yourself about the implications of this step before deciding whether to take it.

Debt reduction approaches. When it comes to mapping out a debt payment plan, it helps to have a strategy in place. Two main strategies you can explore are the Debt Snowball Method (Ramsey Solution, 2024) and the Debt Avalanche Method (Investopedia, 2024). You can find links to more detailed information about these approaches on our book website. The Debt Snowball Method involves listing your debts from smallest to largest based on the amount of the debt you owe. You continue to pay the minimum payments on all debts and then allocate any extra money toward the smallest debt until it's paid off. For example, if you have three debts in the amounts of $200, $2,000, and $20,000, you would start first with the $200 debt and pay that off in full first. Then, you move on to the next smallest debt, using the money you put toward the previous debt to add to your payments on the new one. The Debt Snowball Method can provide a mental boost when you see your debts getting eliminated one by one, so this can be a motivating strategy for many people.

On the other hand, the Debt Avalanche Method focuses on listing your debts from the highest interest rate to the lowest, regardless of the amount of each debt. You continue to pay the minimum on all debts but allocate any extra funds toward the debt with the highest interest rate. Once that debt is paid off, you move to the debt with the next highest interest rate, and so on. This method minimizes the amount of interest paid overall, potentially saving you money on interest in the long run compared to the Debt Snowball Method.

Both approaches have advantages and limitations, and the choice between them depends on your financial situation and goals. Some people prefer the mental boost of paying off smaller debts first (Debt Snowball), while others prefer a focus on saving on interest payments (Debt Avalanche). It's important to research and understand these methods thoroughly before deciding which one best aligns with your needs and preferences.

Of course, while these structured approaches exist, not everyone follows just one method exactly. In your situation, you may find trying some form of variation or combination of these approaches useful. For instance, you might prioritize a particular debt because it's causing significant stress or strain in relationships, such as money borrowed from a family member. Feel free to use a strategy that matches your own needs and preferences. What's most important is that you have a plan you feel confident in following.

A long-term vision for your relationship with debt. In the bigger picture, we encourage you to consider your overall approach and values regarding future debt. Some financial experts advocate for an utterly debt-free lifestyle, viewing any form of debt as unfavorable. Other financial advisors differentiate between "good debt" and "bad debt." The term, "bad debt," is often associated with high interest rates that can chip away at your wealth, such as credit card debt. In contrast, the term, "good debt," often means lower-interest rate loans like student loans or mortgages that enable you to pursue significant goals, while also using other money that's freed up by having the loan to generate returns through investments.

Ultimately, your debt decisions will depend on your unique circumstances and belief systems. Reflect on your values, lifestyle preferences, and what managing debt responsibly means to you. Each person's situation and comfort level with debt is different, and you can feel empowered to develop an approach to managing debt that feels right and manageable to you.

During times of intense stress and rebuilding—such as in the process of starting over after an abusive relationship—it's not uncommon to find yourself needing to take on additional debt. While the thought of accumulating more debt can be disheartening, especially if you're already dealing with financial stress or have a limited income, there are situations that survivors might face that may make this necessary.

For instance, if you're wrapped up in a legal battle with your abuser and require legal representation but lack the financial means to pay your attorney fees with cash, you may have to consider options like taking on debt or negotiating a payment plan with your attorney's office. In such challenging and complex circumstances, seek guidance from trusted advisors or an accountability partner who can assist you in making informed financial decisions.

Dealing with debt can pose significant challenges for survivors of abusive relationships, so approach this topic with careful consideration. Be patient if it takes longer than you'd like to pay down any debts you have, and process any emotions related to your debts in healthy ways. Seek information about your credit records and help from credible, supportive community resources as you develop and implement a plan for navigating debt, both now and throughout your healing journey.

Financial Well-Being Tool #6:

Saving and Investing Strategies

Navigating debt can be complex and challenging, so the previous section may have felt like a bit of a downer. Now, let's shift our focus to a topic that we hope will be at least a little more uplifting: building wealth through savings and investments.

In this section, we'll explore saving and investing strategies. Earlier in this chapter, we discussed types of bank accounts, like savings accounts, checking accounts, money market funds, and CDs. Here, we'll zoom out from specific account types and encourage you to develop an intentional overall approach to saving. We'll also explore helpful savings principles that you might eventually transition into investment opportunities when the time is right and if you wish to do so.

Remember that, in all areas of your financial recovery journey from past abuse, it's perfectly okay to start small and proceed at your own pace. Understand that at this moment, you may not be able to save much, or even at all, especially if you're facing major expenses like legal fees during a court case or dealing with significant debt.

As we discussed earlier, a fundamental financial principle involves aiming to live within your means whenever possible. Throughout this book, we've emphasized that as a survivor of abuse, your financial situation may be complex and challenging. You might have limited or no income, making it difficult to live within your means right now. However, aiming to keep your expenses within the level of your income whenever possible can be a transformative guideline to follow. Any extra money between your income and necessary expenses can be directed toward your financial goals, such as savings or future investments.

It's wise to start small and focus on achievable action plans when saving and investing. Transitioning from spending more than your income and accumulating more debt each month to reaching a break-even point where your income matches your expenses is a significant step. Even saving a small amount, like $5, is worth celebrating. Remember, progress is progress, even when it feels small, and taking even tiny steps toward your financial goals is significant.

Celebrating even minor progress is helpful because it recognizes that you're developing positive financial habits. Saving $5 this month might evolve into saving $50 in a future month, eventually saving $500 monthly or even more. The fundamental principles of saving and investing apply whether you're dealing with small amounts of money or big ones, which highlights the importance of consistency and gradually increasing your savings over time.

Starting on a path toward savings can be frustrating. It's common to feel like you can't make progress, especially when finances are tight. For example, you might diligently save $10 each month and accumulate $100 in savings, only to face an unexpected expense like a car breakdown that wipes out your savings. This cycle of setbacks can be discouraging, but setbacks are often a necessary but challenging part of the healing journey.

Building and consistently using positive financial habits, even if setbacks occur, is important. In the example above, wiping out that $100 in savings is frustrating, but if you didn't have that $100, you'd likely be in a worse position that might have led to accumulating $100 more in debt. So, while setbacks can be frustrating, they're a natural part of the growing process.

As you move along your financial journey and become more intentional and knowledgeable about your finances, it's common to face initial setbacks. However, staying consistent and adhering to your financial principles and values can lead to progress over time. While it may be frustrating initially, maintaining a positive mindset and practicing self-compassion is critical during challenging times. Instead of giving up after setbacks, remind yourself that consistency and seeking new opportunities, such as increasing your income, can keep you on track for positive results in the long run.

Strategies for Saving

In this section, we'll review some specific savings strategies. Overall, you might have different savings goals, such as saving an emergency fund and for a specific purchase you're planning, and allocate your savings across one or more savings accounts. As we review the savings strategies below, consider which ones might be useful to you based on your current and future goals.

Emergency savings funds. Financial experts often recommend building an emergency fund as one of the most important priorities in savings. An emergency fund is a safety net for unexpected challenges, expenses, and financial emergencies.

Many financial experts suggest saving an emergency fund equal to three to six months' worth of essential expenses. However, depending on your circumstances, such as having an unstable job, being the sole provider for a large family, or working in a field with limited job opportunities in your community, you might consider extending this fund to cover up to 12 months of expenses or even more.

The target amount to save in an emergency fund should be based on your essential expenses, not necessarily your total income. For instance, if your annual income is $60,000 but your essential expenses amount to $40,000 yearly, then a six-month emergency fund would be $20,000. To determine the right amount for your emergency fund, carefully review your budget, identify necessary expenses, and exclude discretionary spending or extra savings from the calculation.

Some financial advisors (e.g., Ramsey Solutions, n.d.) recommend starting with a smaller emergency fund, such as $1,000, before focusing on bigger debt repayment goals and then building a fully funded emergency fund with the goal of three to six months of expenses after your debts have been paid off. Others suggest simultaneously building a full emergency fund while paying down debt. Choose a strategy that aligns with your financial goals, feels achievable, and positions you well, given your circumstances.

While having an emergency fund is important, financial experts also often suggest having an upper limit on how much money to keep in a basic savings account that typically offers a low interest rate. Once you've hit your target amount for an emergency fund, you might be ready to start allocating money toward other financial goals or strategies, such as saving for a down payment on a house or starting to invest.

Finally, we recommend establishing rules and systems for when and how you'll let yourself tap into your emergency fund. Whenever possible, reserve this fund for urgent and critical expenses like unexpected car repairs affecting your ability to work, medical emergencies, or job loss rather than discretionary spending. Ideally, if you have some guidelines in place for what you define as an emergency situation, it will make it easier to make decisions about when you might tap into your emergency savings fund.

"Sinking" savings funds. A sinking fund, or a rolling fund, is a way to set money aside for anticipated but irregular expenses that may not be part of your monthly budget, but that you still can anticipate in advance. These expenses might include once-yearly bills, home repairs, birthday gifts, vacations, or holiday spending. Unlike an emergency

fund covering unexpected emergencies, a sinking fund is for planned expenses that occur irregularly throughout the year.

Managing a sinking fund involves setting aside a portion of your regular income to cover categories of anticipated, but irregular, expenses. You can keep track of your sinking fund using a tool like a spreadsheet, where you can list amounts of money for specific categories such as taxes, home repairs, or vacation spending. This approach helps you avoid financial stress when these more significant expenses arise, as you've regularly set money aside for them.

For example, if you're a homeowner, you might expect occasional larger expenses like replacing an appliance that breaks. By adding savings for possible home repairs to a sinking fund each month, you can prepare for these costs in hopes of avoiding the shock of significant, unexpected expenses when these repairs arise. Similarly, setting aside money for holiday spending in a sinking fund can help reduce financial stress during the holiday season.

Sinking funds are a practical way to handle planned expenses outside your regular monthly budget, making them a valuable savings tool for covering irregular but expected costs.

Goal-specific savings funds. Saving for specific goals is another important aspect of financial planning. This type of savings can be part of your sinking fund or a separate account dedicated to a particular goal. For instance, you might be saving for a down payment on a house or to purchase a new car because your current one is getting old and breaking down more often.

Plan for how much of your income you can allocate toward specific savings goals, and account for these savings in your monthly budget allocations. For example, you may allocate $100 per month to your sinking fund and $100 per month toward your home down payment funds. Aligning your savings strategies with your budgeting goals can help you work toward achieving your bigger financial goals.

Picking the right savings account(s) for your goals. Choose saving strategies and accounts that suit your needs and habits. For instance, if you think you'd be tempted to dip into your emergency savings for non-emergency situations, consider keeping it in a separate account or even at a different bank altogether. This separation can make accessing the funds for non-emergency purposes less tempting. Additionally, choosing a higher-yield interest account for your emergency fund, especially if you don't frequently touch it, can be a wise approach.

Saving is a fundamental aspect of financial well-being. Having plans for building and managing your savings can help you move toward more financial empowerment and freedom as you prepare to meet some of life's unexpected (and sometimes expensive!) challenges.

Strategies for Investing

Whether and when to start investing—such as in the stock market or other investments like real estate—depends on your financial situation, risk tolerance, and goals. One consideration involves deciding whether to start investing if you have any debt. Focusing on paying debt off before you start investing might be a wise decision if you have high-interest consumer debt or other substantial debt that is causing you distress. However, other people choose to start investing even while they have some debt, especially if their debt has low interest rates and they have sufficient emergency savings. Financial experts have differing opinions on this matter. Some advisors suggest waiting to invest until your debt has been paid off and you have a solid emergency fund in place. Other advisors recommend starting investing sooner. Again, this is a personal decision.

In general, we prefer a more cautious approach of focusing first on paying down as much debt as possible and building up some initial savings (e.g., an emergency fund) before doing too much in the investing arena. The added risks involved in investing could lead to added stress while navigating the ups and downs of healing from an abusive relationship. However, this is a personal preference, so make comfortable decisions for yourself here. Indeed, there are many different types of investing. As we'll cover more fully in the next chapter, you could even consider spending money to further your education or professional training as an investment (in yourself)!

When making decisions about investing, think about your own goals and financial situation. For instance, investing in a retirement fund at work, where you could miss out on an employer match by not investing, might be a wise decision, even while you are paying down some of your debts. As always, we encourage focusing on your unique goals, understanding your individual situation, and educating yourself on your options. Investing is a highly personalized process, so prioritize what feels comfortable. Remember that investing almost always involves some level of risk, ranging from relatively lower-risk investments like broad-based index funds to more speculative ones like cryptocurrency. So, factor your level of risk tolerance into your investing decisions as well.

Let's walk through some investment accounts that might make sense for you.

Retirement investments. When it comes to retirement savings, there are several options to consider. If you're employed, you may have access to a 401(k) plan, a 403(b) plan, and/or a 457 plan. Employer-sponsored retirement investment funds often provide tax advantages. Other retirement account options, such as a SEP IRA or a solo 401(k), are available for self-employed people.

Alternatively, you can explore individual retirement accounts (IRAs), which can be traditional or Roth, depending on your tax preferences and financial goals. With a Roth IRA, for instance, your contributions are taxed up front, allowing your investments to grow tax-free, and you won't pay taxes on withdrawals in retirement.

Retirement funds can be a precious resource for your future, and having time on your side is extremely helpful in retirement planning. Unfortunately, frequent news headlines today highlight how many people today need to catch up on their retirement savings. Retirement pension plans used to be more common among employers. These plans require a set number of years (e.g., 30 years) of work to become fully vested, and then provide monthly income for the rest of the retiree's life and possibly their spouse's life, depending on the plan. However, with the decline in pension plans, individuals have more responsibility to focus on their retirement planning to secure their financial future during retirement.

A full discussion of retirement planning is beyond the scope of this book, so we encourage you to consider seeking out more credible information to help you plan for your retirement over time. We've included some resources on our book website (www.sourceforsurvivors.info/financialabuse) as a starting point.

Focusing on retirement savings can be challenging, especially when your likely retirement date is decades away. However, adopting a mindset that prioritizes savings early on can be beneficial. Let's briefly discuss the concept of compounding interest here.

In the context of debt, interest works against you because you're paying it to your debtor, who is gaining financially by earning your interest. However, when it comes to investing, including for your retirement, the power of interest, particularly compounding interest over time, can work in your favor. This is where you start to hear about the idea of your money making money. If you invest $1,000 and earn 10% interest in a year ($100), and then if you leave the total of $1,100 in the investment for the next year, the interest will be accruing based on the $1,100. Over time, this can lead to significant growth in your investments (assuming they continue to earn positive interest over time).

Compounding interest from investments means that your earnings can grow exponentially over time (although of course, there's also a risk that investments might lose value over time, especially with higher-risk investments and during economic downturns). Earning interest differs from debt, where compounding interest works against you, enriching others at your expense. Learning about the concept of compounding interest is valuable because when you invest, time becomes your friend. Investing even smaller amounts early in your life and allowing them to grow over time can be incredibly valuable for building long-term wealth.

Other types of investments. Other investments to consider may include college funds and general (i.e., non-retirement) investment accounts, such as taxable investment accounts offered by brokerage firms. More speculative investments include cryptocurrencies. Real estate can be another form of investing, although it can be labor-intensive, especially if you're directly managing properties and acting as a landlord.

Like many aspects of life, investing can be as simple or complex as you choose to make it. Investing inherently carries risks, so it's important to know your level of risk tolerance, both emotionally and financially. Longer-term investment strategies, such as a "buy and hold" approach, are generally wise, although it's also smart to avoid holding onto bad investments (once you can tell they are bad!) for too long.

This section provided only a basic introduction to investing, so if you're interested in including investing in your financial plan, consider consulting credible sources of information or working with a trusted investment advisor. Understanding yourself and crafting a plan that instills a sense of security is valuable when it comes to savings and investing. Committing to this plan, even with seemingly small steps, is key to achieving financial stability over time. Continue learning and building habits that can grow stronger as your financial circumstances improve and stabilize.

Financial Well-Being Tool #7:

Giving and Generosity

Let's briefly discuss another aspect of financial well-being that may or may not align with your priorities: giving back and generosity. For many individuals, sharing resources with loved ones, supporting charitable causes, or contributing to faith communities holds significant value. Some may even view giving as a spiritual practice, such as the practice of tithing in Judeo-Christian traditions.

We're not here to make value judgments about whether or not you *should* include a focus on giving in your financial planning. We believe there are various ways to express generosity beyond direct financial contributions, such as volunteering time or providing emotional support to others.

That said, we invite you to reflect on what generosity means to you and whether and how you envision incorporating financial giving into your life. Consider how your financial goals and practices can align with your values around generosity and giving, whether through financial donations or other forms of support.

Ultimately, decisions related to giving and generosity are deeply personal. Reflect on what giving means to you, whether and how you wish to practice generosity, and its role in your current and future financial plans. Below, for those who are rebuilding their finances after an abusive relationship, we have a few suggestions if you're thinking about integrating giving into your overall journey.

First, recognize that while giving can be meaningful, setting boundaries is important to prevent potentially negative impacts on your finances. If you feel that providing financial support to others would strain your finances, declining or postponing such gifts until you're in a more stable financial position is reasonable.

Second, we advise caution when lending money to friends or family members. While you may want to help, consider the potential strain that loaning money may place on your relationships. Establishing clear guidelines for yourself can be beneficial. For instance, you might establish a personal policy of not lending money to anyone but staying open to sharing resources as gifts. This approach can help to avoid misunderstandings and provide a more positive, sustainable way to support others.

In addition, empower yourself to make giving-related decisions that align with your values and priorities. Giving should be meaningful and voluntary. In the context of the "Paying It Forward" Commitment in the Pathway for Survivors model that we reviewed in Chapter 4, survivors of abusive relationships often find fulfillment in helping others who have experienced similar challenges. This could involve supporting individuals currently in abusive relationships or those who have recently left such situations.

However, paying it forward does not resonate with all survivors, and that's perfectly okay. Engaging with organizations or individuals addressing abusive relationships can sometimes be triggering or upsetting due to memories. Remember that you're not obligated to share your story publicly or donate to domestic violence organizations to validate your healing journey as a survivor of an abusive relationship. Your healing and authenticity are valid regardless of your involvement in such activities. If contributing to these causes is meaningful for you, it can be a valuable part of your healing process, but it's entirely your choice.

Finally, as you become more stable in your finances and have additional resources, consider establishing guidelines or practices aligned with your financial goals if you wish to make giving and generosity a regular part of your financial plan. For instance, you might adopt a practice like tithing, or giving 10% of your income, if it resonates with you. Alternatively, you could set a different percentage for giving that feels more meaningful or reflects your values. Whether allocating a certain percentage of your income or donating to specific causes, setting personally meaningful guidelines ensures that your giving aligns with your financial well-being and overall goals.

In conclusion, giving and generosity can be meaningful as you progress along your financial recovery journey. Still, it is important to do so in ways that feel right for you and don't compromise your financial stability.

Conclusion

Overall, we encourage you to remain open to adapting and evolving your financial plans and strategies over time. Your values and priorities are likely to change as you grow and experience different seasons of life, and it's important to be flexible and responsive to these shifts. As you take steps toward healing richer and building a prosperous financial future, anticipate growth and opportunities that may arise unexpectedly. Even during challenging economic times, practicing reasonable financial management strategies can offer a strong foundation for your future well-being.

Throughout this book, we've emphasized that financial well-being and prosperity mean different things to each person. As you continue to learn and refine your financial skills, continue to align your financial decisions with your personal goals and aspirations. By staying mindful, adaptable, and committed to your financial journey, you can create your unique path toward a fulfilling and secure financial future that reflects your values and dreams.

Chapter 9

Exploring Career and Educational Pathways

Chapter 8 covered financial investments like savings accounts, the stock market, and even real estate. However, have you ever considered your own personal and professional development as another important investment you can make with your time, energy, and resources (financial and otherwise)? We are confident of this: *you* are one of the best investments you can make along the journey of recovering from past abuse.

There are many ways to invest in yourself. These include prioritizing self-care, nurturing your physical well-being by getting enough rest, and dedicating time to your mental health and healing. You can also invest in yourself by devoting time, energy, and resources to uplifting activities, supportive relationships, and meaningful goals.

Our focus in this chapter is on a specific type of investing in yourself: investing in educational and career development opportunities. We recognize readers are likely in many different circumstances related to their education and careers. Some readers are likely already doing work they love that provides them with the income they need, others might be very unhappy or unfulfilled in their current jobs, and still others have unique circumstances that mean paid work is not needed right now (e.g., being retired, caregiving for a family member, or having enough financial resources through an inheritance or trust fund). Depending on your unique circumstances, the information in this chapter may be more or less relevant to you.

However, even if you don't have immediate concerns about your educational or career status, remember that life situations can change, and your interests or needs may shift over time. Also in this chapter, we invite you to think beyond narrow definitions of education and jobs. We encourage all readers to reflect on *learning* and *working* more broadly, whether that looks like becoming a lifelong learner, working in paid or unpaid roles, and considering your values around careers and education.

Our main goal in this chapter is to discuss how exploring new learning and working opportunities could support your personal growth, enhance your financial well-being, and contribute to your overall abuse recovery journey. As we discussed earlier in this book, many survivors face challenges in their educational and career pursuits due to the effects of the abuse, including instances of career and educational abuse directly perpetrated by the abuser. Also, the control dynamics within abusive relationships can lead survivors to become hindered in their career trajectories, such as if their abusers limited their career options during the relationship or chipped away at their confidence related to work or educational goals.

In addition, the financial effects of an abusive relationship might contribute to a heightened sense of urgency to increase your income, and work-related income often plays a big part in people's overall financial picture. No matter where you are currently in your educational and career pathways, taking time for self-reflection can be helpful. Working and learning can play significant roles in our lives. For example, people working a full-time job spend much time engaged in their work and interacting with their coworkers. The quality of our jobs and workplace cultures can significantly impact our overall quality of life.

Reflecting on your current career path can lead to a renewed sense of purpose and direction, even if you realize you don't want to make any changes now and are happy where you are. However, considering the time many of us spend at work each week, regular self-reflection about our work and learning opportunities is very meaningful.

Your educational and career goals and aspirations may evolve along your abuse recovery journey. You might not feel like you can make changes right now. Or, you might be raring to go and brimming with excitement about having a newfound sense of freedom and empowerment to explore different paths and opportunities that didn't seem possible before within the confines of your relationship.

Eileen's career story is a testament to the transformative power of pursuing educational and career goals during the healing journey. Please read below for Eileen's reflections about how her academic and career journey contributed significantly to her healing and self-discovery.

After leaving my relationship, I felt lost and terrified, overwhelmed by the question, "Now what?" I found myself in my 40s as a former stay-at-home mother with the freedom to make my own choices, but I struggled profoundly with the confidence to make decisions and even to know what I wanted to do with my life after the abuse I experienced. With only one semester of college completed earlier in my life, I was starting from scratch.

What I did know was that I owed a significant part of my healing to my weekly therapy sessions. Therapy was the first place where I felt safe enough to share my abuse history. It was in therapy that I discovered I wasn't to blame for the abuse I experienced. Therapy provided hope. I felt validated as I unpacked my story, and I began to think about how I could help others who had experienced abuse. I started to feel more empowered and wanted to share that with others.

To make a long story short, I eventually decided to go back to school to become a therapist. I remember the excitement and anxiety I felt walking into the college for the first time. Writing my admission essay felt paralyzing because of the deep self-doubt and the persistent feeling that I wasn't smart enough. Abuse can leave you with severe self-doubt and a lack of trust in yourself, and I felt that deeply. Yet, something in me persisted despite those old narratives.

On the first day of school, I walked a few steps on campus, only to turn around and start to head back to my car as waves of memories of verbal and emotional abuse flooded my mind, triggering panic. But at that moment, I took the most significant leap of faith in myself. I turned back around, walked into my first class, and spent the following several semesters attempting to prove to myself that I was smart enough. I took chances by speaking up in class and sharing my point of view. With each small act of courage, I healed a little more and let go of having to prove anything.

I thrived in school due to positive feedback from my professors, peer support, and a great deal of tutoring to help me fill the time gap from my first college experience. I went on to earn my Master's degree and fulfill my dream of becoming a therapist supporting survivors. I started my private practice to focus on my purpose–giving back. By sharing a small part of my story, I hope to convey the importance of putting one foot in front of the other and stepping out of fear rather than letting it prevent you from finding your version of success, meaning, and purpose. Each time we show up for ourselves in small ways, we move closer to freedom. Our failures lead to new understandings, and we become more comfortable making decisions. Healing is a long journey but the only path to true freedom. Christine and I believe in every person's ability to be successful through the healing journey and finding financial freedom.

Eileen's experiences highlight the growth and empowerment that can stem from pursuing career and educational goals along the healing journey. Her story is a shining example of how personal growth and professional development can intersect, leading to meaningful transformation and important contributions to the world around her.

Of course, each person's journey is unique, and there's no one-size-fits-all approach to recovery and empowerment, including in work and learning. Remember to personalize your journey and apply the insights and guidance from this book in ways that resonate with your own experiences and goals.

We'll begin this chapter by exploring general ideas about creating a vision and plan for your education and career, starting with self-reflection on your meaning and motivations for learning and working. Afterward, we'll discuss strategies for approaching your educational and career development. We'll then explore strategies for pursuing further education if that aligns with your journey. Finally, we'll discuss tools, resources, and strategies tailored to those seeking career guidance or considering career changes.

Reflecting on Your Meaning and Motivation Behind Learning and Working

We invite you to reflect on the personal meaning and motivation behind learning and working. This kind of self-reflection is useful because work and learning take up significant space in people's lives. For survivors, these aspects of life can play a key role in the abuse recovery process, especially when they help pave the pathway to greater financial well-being and independence.

There are many reasons why people engage in work and learning, and we'll explore some of these motivations below. For many people, a primary motivation for work is to generate income that offers security and stability. At a practical level, work can lead to income, which helps us meet basic needs such as paying bills, buying food, and securing housing. Working for compensation is not selfish. Instead, many people must work as a way to afford their own and their family's overall well-being and livelihood.

Beyond the basics of working for pay, other possible motivations inspire people to work. One motivation is the sense of meaning and purpose that work can bring to one's life, whether through paid or unpaid roles. Engaging in work, even if it's on a volunteer basis, that aligns with your values and beliefs can bring a profound sense of fulfillment and purpose. Working can help us feel like we're making a difference in the world and have a sense of calling or mission in our lives.

Relatedly, working can offer meaning through a sense of service and contribution to our community or the broader society. Many people find fulfillment in service-oriented work that positively impacts others' lives. Giving back and making meaningful contributions through work can be incredibly rewarding and fulfilling.

Even if it doesn't directly involve serving others, work can provide a sense of affirmation, contributing to our self-worth and sense of identity. This can happen in various ways, such as feeling accomplished when you master new skills, receiving recognition and appreciation from colleagues or supervisors, and feeling valued for being a reliable and effective team member.

A desire to be a lifelong learner is another possible motivation for working and learning. Continual learning and growth can contribute to ongoing personal development. Whether through formal education or informal learning experiences, gaining new knowledge, skills, and perspectives can be enriching and meaningful.

At a basic level, work also can offer meaningful, interesting ways to spend our time. For many of us, work provides structure to our days, a sense of productivity, and a reason to get up and go in the mornings.

Finally, work can facilitate social connections, friendships, and relationships. Workplaces are often spaces where people interact, collaborate, and build professional and personal relationships. These connections can be valuable in providing support, networking opportunities, and a sense of belonging.

These are just some reasons and motivations why people may work or seek out learning opportunities. We invite you to take time to reflect on the following questions:

- *What are the reasons that working and learning matter to you?*

- *How, if at all, do you see your work and learning goals as being related to your overall abuse recovery process?*

- *What would it mean to you to pursue new goals or opportunities in your career and education?*

Keep these reflections in mind as you move forward in this chapter, and especially as you consider specific educational or career goals you might want to pursue. During your healing journey, you have the opportunity for self-reflection and the freedom to explore pathways that are meaningful to you.

Pursuing new educational or career goals can be difficult, especially if you're still grappling with the aftereffects of abuse. However, you are worthy of growing and dreaming, and your growth in these areas can benefit your healing journey immensely. Of course, increasing your income can bring practical benefits toward your financial goals, such as building savings, reducing debt, or investing. In addition, beyond the tangible benefits, there's potential value in gaining confidence, pride, and a sense of self-worth by setting and achieving career and educational goals. This newfound confidence can positively impact other areas of your life, including your mental health and overall recovery from abuse.

As you consider what new directions you might take, you may find yourself rediscovering buried dreams or creating new ones. We encourage you to revisit Chapter 7, which focuses on dreaming, goal setting, and action planning. You can apply this dream-goal-action planning process to your learning and work pathways to help build short- and long-term goals that are meaningful for you.

In the next section, we share general career and educational development strategies. After that, we'll narrow our focus to explore educational goals in detail before moving onto the topic of career development.

General Strategies to Support Your Educational and Career Development

Here are general strategies to keep in mind as you consider pursuing educational and career development dreams and goals:

Maintain a long-term perspective. Remember that achieving any big-picture dreams and goals will likely take time, possibly years or even decades. Keeping this long-range view in mind can provide direction and motivation to help you keep going even if you don't see immediate results. Progress often happens gradually, so be patient and enjoy the journey, while keeping your long-range goals on the horizon.

Focus on short-term steps, Identify short-term actions that you can take to move forward toward your long-term aspirations. These short-term steps serve as building blocks toward your bigger dreams and goals. You can make consistent progress and stay motivated by breaking down your journey into manageable tasks.

Celebrate your successes. Acknowledge and celebrate both significant milestones and seemingly small achievements along the way. Whether you're working toward completing a degree, landing a new job, receiving a promotion, or launching a new business, big moments are worthy of celebration. However, limiting your celebrations only to major milestones can lead to discouragement. Small successes are worthy of celebration, too! For example, completing an assignment or a course with a satisfactory grade, meeting an important deadline, or contributing meaningfully to a work meeting can all be reasons to celebrate. Taking time to acknowledge and celebrate more minor successes, even if it's just with a moment of recognition or a small celebration, can help you maintain motivation and positivity on your journey.

Learn from setbacks. Mistakes, setbacks, and even failures are a natural part of any career or educational journey. We can grow when we seek to learn from these experiences. It's normal for successful people to have moments they wish they could redo. How you respond and use these experiences as opportunities to learn, grow, and make meaningful changes moving forward matters. Reframing setbacks as lessons can shift your perspective and empower you to move past them.

Focus on the time you have left more than the time that has passed. It's never too late in life to start pursuing new goals and dreams. While there may be societal stereotypes or biases about the "right" timing for certain milestones, such as going to college as a young adult, try to challenge these assumptions. There are no set age limits in many career paths, as discussed in Chapter 7 and Christine's experiences with graduate students of varying ages—even well into traditional retirement ages—pursuing a new career path in the counseling field.

Time continues to pass, regardless of the choices we make. Reflect on where you want to see yourself in the next few years or decades and what goals would bring you fulfillment and meaning. While specific paths may have limitations based on age (almost certainly, it's too late to pursue a professional basketball career in the NBA or WNBA in your 50s), there are often alternative ways to explore interests and achieve goals without strict time constraints. It's about finding what works best for you at your current stage of life. Don't let preconceived notions of age or timing discourage you from pursuing new aspirations.

Surround yourself with supporters. Another valuable strategy is to build a supportive team around you. This team can consist of mentors or advisors who offer guidance and expertise in your chosen path. Additionally, having supporters in your personal life, such as friends or family members who rally behind you, can be incredibly motivating.

Networking with like-minded individuals is also beneficial. For example, if you're venturing into entrepreneurship, joining networking groups for small business owners can provide helpful connections, especially if you can make connections with people who are navigating similar growth stages in their businesses. Similarly, if you're returning to education as a non-traditional student, seeking out resources like adult learner offices on campus can offer tailored support for your needs and goals.

Explore different options within the context of your broader goals. Maintaining a flexible and exploratory mindset is valuable when defining what work and learning look like for you in your life. Many possible pathways might be fulfilling in your professional and educational journeys.

Let's explore an example within the mental health field, which both of us can relate to as professionals in this field. The conventional route to becoming a licensed mental health professional involves pursuing graduate studies, completing clinical hour requirements, and obtaining licensure. However, this pathway can be lengthy and might not be feasible for everyone due to any number of practical constraints or simply not wanting to take so long to enter this field.

In such cases, someone interested in this career path might consider alternative roles within the mental health arena, such as peer support positions for individuals with lived experiences, paraprofessional roles, or administrative roles in mental health agencies. In addition, opportunities exist in mental health organizations in areas like finance, marketing, outreach, and communications.

To take this example even further, making an impact in the mental health arena doesn't always require a paid job in a mental health agency. For instance, you could work in an unrelated job in any field but still contribute to mental health-related causes by serving on a nonprofit board focused on mental health advocacy in your community.

The takeaway is to explore many options and remain open to trying different approaches until you discover the path that resonates most with your aspirations and circumstances. Flexibility and willingness to explore other avenues can lead to finding the right fit for you and achieving your broader goals, even if it means taking an unconventional approach.

Allow your dreams and goals to evolve. Your career plans and goals can be an ever-evolving part of your professional and personal development. In today's seemingly constantly changing world, it's almost expected that your goals and priorities will shift over time, especially as you enter new phases of life, different financial circumstances, or changes in your family's schedule.

Maintaining an open and flexible mindset is helpful not only during the initial stages of your financial abuse recovery process, but also as you navigate your future work and learning journey. An open, flexible mindset involves being grounded in what is meaningful and purposeful for you while remaining open to potential changes and new directions that may emerge as you move forward.

Consider the intersections among work, learning, and financial well-being. Your career, education, and economic well-being are deeply interconnected. Your educational and career pathways can significantly impact your financial situation, especially regarding potential income changes or increases that can affect your financial status.

Be mindful of these intersections along each stage in this journey. You may not currently earn as much as you wish you did, but (whenever possible) living within your means at any phase of your career is helpful. Consider how your work and learning decisions impact your financial health and overall well-being, including your mental health and relationships. Your values will influence these decisions, highlighting the importance of regular reflection to ensure you're on a personally meaningful path in your career, education, and finances.

As you explore new career opportunities or advance in your education or career, you are likely to encounter new people, lifestyles, and pathways. Stay true to your own values and unique journey, avoiding distractions, temptations, or comparisons with others that may lead to unnecessary feelings of jealousy or envy. Regularly check in with yourself to ensure any changes you consider align with what is personally meaningful and relevant for you.

Strategies to Further Your Education and Learning

Formal education, which involves seeking official training like pursuing a degree or specific certifications, can be a valuable, if not essential, part of advancing your career. However, as you explore different career and educational pathways, take time to figure out your career goals and whether formal education, such as a degree or certification program, is necessary or beneficial for your goals.

In many cases, formal education is indeed necessary. As an example, suppose your goal is to become a licensed clinician in the mental health field, such as a Licensed Clinical Social Worker (LCSW), Licensed Marriage and Family Therapist (LMFT), or Licensed Professional Counselor (LPC). In that case, you typically need to have both a bachelor's and a master's degree to be eligible for pursuing such licensure. These degrees provide the required foundational knowledge and skills needed for these professions. There's usually no way around these kinds of educational requirements.

However, not all career paths require formal education to the same extent. Some careers prioritize experience, skills, and certifications over traditional degrees. For instance, specific career fields in technology, creative industries, or entrepreneurship may value practical experience and specialized training more than formal degrees. Whether formal educational requirements are needed for your desired career pathway, keep in mind that learning can happen in many different ways. Ongoing learning—whether required or not—can be a helpful way to build skills that enhance your career and personal growth and development.

There are many ways to advance your education and learning, from formal schooling to informal learning opportunities. Here are some learning options to consider:

- *Formal degrees*: This includes pursuing a traditional academic degree or diploma, such as completing a GED, attending a community college for an associate's degree, earning a bachelor's degree from a four-year institution, or pursuing graduate studies like a master's or doctoral degree.

Specific professional degrees are also available, like a medical doctor (MD) or Juris Doctor (JD) for lawyers.

• *Online learning*: Many open-access online learning platforms offer various courses and certifications. These platforms provide flexibility and convenience for learners. Some are free, whereas others require fees.

• *Reading and independent research*: You may be interested in enhancing your knowledge through online reading materials, including resources from professional associations and books related to your desired field.

• *Job-specific certifications*: Consider pursuing certifications from credentialing organizations relevant to your career goals. These certifications may not be part of a formal degree program but can demonstrate your expertise in specific areas.

• *On-the-job training*: You might want to seek opportunities for on-the-job training, such as apprenticeships or internships, to gain practical skills and experience in your chosen field.

• *Peer support roles and lived experiences*: In peer support roles, certain personal experiences are typically job requirements. For example, peer support roles in the mental health field leverage individuals' experiences to support and guide others.

By exploring a vast array of learning opportunities, you can tailor your learning goals to align with your career goals and personal interests. Evaluate what you need to do based on the requirements of your field, while also considering alternative learning pathways that could enhance your skills and contribute to your professional development. To help clarify possible next steps in your learning journey, consider the following strategies:

First, clarify your career goals. Define your career goals and investigate the typical educational requirements for any roles you're considering. Determine if a degree or certification program is necessary for your desired career.

Second, assess your current skills and experiences. Evaluate your existing skills, knowledge, and expertise. Identify areas where you may need or want additional training or qualifications to achieve your career goals.

Third, explore alternative training options. Investigate alternative training programs, workshops, "boot camps," or online courses that offer relevant skills and certifications in your target industry. These options sometimes provide more targeted and practical learning experiences than traditional degrees.

Fourth, consider career advancement opportunities offered by your current employer. If your workplace offers opportunities for advancement through promotion pathways, additional training, or certifications, explore those options within your organization. This can be a cost-effective way to gain new skills and progress in your career.

Finally, seek guidance and advice. Consult with mentors, career counselors, or professionals in your target industry to gain insights into your chosen field's educational requirements and career paths. These advisors can provide valuable guidance on the most effective educational strategies for reaching your career goals.

By carefully considering these strategies, you can make informed decisions about furthering your education and learning to support your career advancement and financial goals. When exploring educational opportunities, seek credible resources and institutions to learn about your options. By proactively seeking information, understanding any requirements you might face, and seeking supportive connections, you can make informed decisions about your educational journey and align it with your career aspirations.

Paying for further education. Understanding how to pay for further educational expenses, when applicable, requires careful planning. Here are some key points to consider. First, be mindful of how you plan to finance your education, exploring options such as scholarships, grants, fellowships, and saving money before pursuing a degree. Second, reflect on your comfort level with assuming educational debt and consider ways to minimize long-term financial burdens. Then, seek resources and information through educational institutions' financial aid offices. Government programs also may offer financial aid options, but it's important to understand the differences between student loans, scholarships, and grants.

Consult with trusted financial advisors or accountability partners to review your options when making education-related financial decisions. They can provide valuable insights and help you make informed choices that align with your financial goals. Also, consider how pursuing education may impact your employment and related income, such as adjusting your work schedule or choosing programs with flexible class options to accommodate your work schedule.

Avoid over-committing financially to educational pursuits without considering your income, expenses, and long-term financial stability whenever possible. Carefully evaluate the potential impact of educational costs on your overall economic well-being. By approaching education financing with mindfulness, seeking guidance, and making informed decisions, you can pursue educational opportunities that enhance your skills and knowledge while factoring in your financial health and stability.

Restarting progress toward a previous educational pathway. If you're considering restarting a degree program you started in the past but never completed, gather information and resources to position yourself effectively for this opportunity. For instance, if you completed credits from a college program that was interrupted due to your abuser's actions, you can explore options to apply those credits toward completing your degree.

Many college campuses have dedicated offices to support adult or transfer students. Within these offices, advisors often can review your prior credits and provide guidance on whether your previous coursework can apply to a new degree program. Not all colleges accept older or transfer credits, so seeking this information early on can help you make informed decisions about your educational path. However, many institutions accept transfer credits from accredited institutions, even if they were earned some time ago. This information can be extremely valuable in shaping your educational goals and plans moving forward.

Another reminder about the importance of patience. Pursuing new educational goals can be a journey that requires time and patience. Seeking a degree or entering a professional training program, especially when you have many other responsibilities demanding your time, can take a significant amount of time. Honor your progress and be patient with yourself and your unique journey. Celebrate your progress, understanding that achieving your educational goals may require time and dedication.

Strategies for Furthering Your Career Pathways

If you have dreams for big or small career changes, seek support and gather information to help you make these career moves. In this final section of this chapter, we'll cover tools, resources, and steps you can take as you consider potential career changes. Your needs may vary depending on where you currently stand in your career journey. Some readers may be early in figuring out your desired career path, while others may know exactly what you want to pursue next. At every stage of your process, various types of support are available, and many career strategies can be beneficial throughout the process.

Seek career information and guidance. A valuable resource when exploring career options is to engage in career counseling, assessments, or other related services. These resources can be beneficial as you consider specific challenges or circumstances you may be facing. For instance, if you're still trying to figure out your career goals, assessments are available to help identify your strengths, interests, and potential career fits. You can visit our book's website (www.sourceforsurvivors.info/financialabuse) for links to these resources and more information about these assessments. Many career-related books, like the classic *'What Color Is Your Parachute?'* by Richard N. Bolles, can offer helpful insights.

Whether or not you have a clear picture of what you'd like the next phase of your career to look like, another helpful resource can be connecting with a career counselor or a career coach. If you're interested in speaking with someone who can assist you with career counseling, you could take a few possible directions. The National Career Development Association (https://www.ncda.org) is a founding division of the American Counseling Association that focuses on career counseling. Their website includes a searchable database for finding career counselors in local communities. Other career counseling and support resources may be available to you, whether in your local community or from a college or university you attended previously. Sometimes, these institutions make their career counseling centers available to alumni and other community members. Additionally, local nonprofits might offer job skills training, workforce development, and career advising and coaching.

Spend time exploring resources available in your community or state. Local employment-related agencies, business development agencies, economic development agencies, and community organizations like the Chamber of Commerce often take a keen interest in workforce development. They often offer resources for career development, professional networking, and job skills training.

Explore career and networking opportunities. There are many ways to explore different career pathways and opportunities. One way to find information is by searching online about various career fields and employers. Websites like Indeed or Glassdoor provide ratings from past and present employees, which can help assess work culture. However, these ratings are sometimes skewed toward negative perspectives, so try to seek out other information sources to supplement the initial information that you find.

Reading and learning about different career fields can offer insights if you're considering a job move. Conducting informational interviews is another valuable approach. This involves reaching out to someone working in a field, asking for a little bit of their time (e.g., 30 minutes), and asking about their experiences, likes, dislikes, and the steps needed for success in that field. Networking events, conferences, and training programs, both local and online, also can be beneficial for making connections and gathering information.

Social media platforms like LinkedIn offer opportunities to build connections, search for job opportunities, join interest groups, and learn from leaders in the career field you hope to join. Seeking mentorship or guidance is also valuable, whether through educational mentors like professors or teachers or through mentors in your field or chosen career path. Mentors can provide helpful advice and support as you navigate your career journey.

Building self-advocacy and negotiation skills. Practicing negotiation and self-advocacy skills can help you to develop and advance in your career. These skills can be beneficial in many ways. While many job-related negotiations often revolve around salary increases during hiring or while in a job, having a broader perspective on advocacy and negotiation in the workplace is helpful. Here are a few examples of other possible job-related points for negotiation: better work-life balance, tuition reimbursement for further education, a flexible schedule to accommodate new training, job shadowing opportunities in other areas of the company, and opportunities for career growth within a current job.

For survivors of past abuse, advocating for oneself and negotiating may feel uncomfortable and require time and patience to learn. In abusive relationships, there is often little room for self-advocacy or healthy communication. While we can only scratch the surface about the topics of negotiation and self-advocacy in this book, we provide resources and links on our website (www.sourceforsurvivors.info/financialabuse) for further information and opportunities to enhance these skills.

Consider the context of societal changes in how people work. The world of work has been evolving in recent years. In past generations, people approached work differently, often staying with one company throughout their careers. Today, however, the world of work has become much more flexible and diverse, offering various income-generating pathways. These include traditional W-2 employment (full-time or part-time), the "gig" economy, entrepreneurship, contract work, and freelancing. While this diversity offers flexibility and options, it can also be overwhelming. A helpful strategy is to reflect on some key questions:

- *What type of work most appeals to you now and in the future?*

- *What income level do you need? What type(s) of work align with your income needs?*

- *What work formats align with your goals and desired lifestyle?*

Consider both/and perspectives, meaning you may find that different approaches work well for you currently and over time. Many people in today's world combine various sources of income or have side hustles alongside traditional employment. Diversifying your income streams can promote your financial well-being, especially in volatile economic times. Consider the advantages and disadvantages of each option, be mindful of tax implications, and assess how each choice aligns with your overall goals and values.

Short- and long-term career planning: The last strategy we'll cover here regarding pursuing new directions in your career is to map out a specific short- and long-term plan to get from where you are now to where you want to go. This involves revisiting the points discussed in previous chapters, particularly around dreaming, goal setting, and action planning in Chapter 7. Be as specific as possible in outlining your plans, and seek out different resources and information to help fill in the blanks and steps along those pathways.

The financial opportunities connected to new career pathways can be a game-changer for improving your financial situation, although money is not the only factor to consider. Think about all aspects of work that are meaningful and important to you. For example, at some point, you may decide to pursue a lower-paying job that aligns more with your values and interests. Reflect, plan, and believe in yourself as you navigate your career goals and see what exciting opportunities await you.

Conclusion

This chapter covered the role that learning and work play in our financial well-being and our sense of meaning and purpose in life. We hope the insights shared in this chapter sparked ideas about your goals and possible next steps in education and career, including how these areas might become part of your healing journey post-abuse. Navigating educational and career pathways often feels like a winding journey, so it's important to practice patience at each stage while looking forward to your future goals. It's natural for goals and pathways to evolve as you learn, grow, and discover new opportunities and connections.

Learning and working are intertwined with our overall quality of life, including along the abuse recovery journey. Lingering effects of the abusive relationship may surface, such as self-doubt or memories of your abuser's criticism. Continue to navigate these challenges with strategies like counseling, mentoring, journaling, and self-validation. As much as possible, try to stay focused on your goals, and don't allow your history with abuse to stand in the way of your confidence or worthiness to pursue meaningful goals.

We encourage you to dream as big as you'd like in your career and education as a powerful way to empower yourself along your healing journey. Your personal goals in these areas can offer opportunities to continue building your resilience, growth, and sense of purpose and direction in life.

Chapter 10

Conclusion: Overcoming Past Abuse and Building a Solid Foundation for Your Future

You've reached the final chapter of this book. We celebrate your intentionality and progress in reading and applying the information in this book. Take a moment to pause and acknowledge the steps you took as you read through the chapters. Hopefully, you've gained deeper insight into the dynamics of abusive relationships and how they intersect with survivors' financial well-being. We also hope you've learned information that helps you understand the often long and complicated journey of financial abuse recovery.

Our intention for this book has been to offer information and practical strategies to help you examine your current financial well-being and start planning and moving toward a future that brings greater economic independence and freedom. Our wish for our readers is that you feel more empowered to begin to set and work toward goals and dreams that will help you to experience stability, peace, healing, and thriving. We believe that survivors can not only heal, but *heal richer* and experience abundance and joy in their lives. This final chapter will tie everything together with some final encouragement for you as you continue your healing journey. We'll also review key takeaway messages we hope will stay with you long after you've finished this book.

Embracing Your Healing Journey

As we've explored throughout these pages, there are many connections between experiencing an abusive relationship and the financial well-being of victims and survivors. We firmly believe that healing and recovery from abuse are both possible and achievable. Through our own experiences and collective work with countless survivors, we've witnessed firsthand how seemingly small steps toward healing can significantly impact survivors' overall well-being and the healing journey.

Regardless of any past or current experiences that created challenges in your finances or other areas of life, we want to remind you—and encourage you to remind yourself—that *you are worthy of a brighter future. Yes, you*.

You are worthy of good things in your life. *You* are worthy of feeling safe and secure. This includes a sense of safety and security in your finances, but it extends to all areas of your life. Although, likely, we don't know you personally, we know enough about what you've been through as a survivor to know that you deserve a brighter future—despite what you may have been told or led to feel by your abuser. By now, we hope you've seen that your abuser's credibility is quite questionable. They intended to harm and control you, not to offer you help, support, and encouragement. Their words may still ring out loudly in your mind, but please continue to work to let your own needs, voice, and wisdom become stronger and more overpowering than the lies your abuser told you.

Even if you feel overwhelmed, sad, or traumatized by what happened to you, know that you can take steps forward in your life, seek support, and build meaningful, healthy relationships that will help you move toward your dreams and goals. This is true even if your goals and dreams have become deeply buried within you or if your abuser tried to convince you that they aren't possible.

As we discussed throughout this book, your abuser likely was intent on inflicting significant harm on you through their actions, seeking power and control over you. However, remember that their words and behaviors do not have to define you. The abusive things they said about you were not true and were not intended to support or care for you as a caring, supportive partner should.

It may not be easy to believe that a brighter future is possible. Still, as you continue taking steps toward your future and develop a vision for what it could look like, you likely will begin to believe more in the possibility of that future as you see it unfolding. It won't always be easy. The healing journey has been quite challenging for both of us in our own lives. However, as we've overcome challenge after challenge, we have seen with greater clarity the positive future that has emerged over time.

Financial Well-Being in the Context of the Broader Healing Journey

Right now, your finances might be your top priority at this stage of your healing journey. However, it's also possible that other priorities and needs related to your healing are taking precedence. Whatever the case, we encourage you to feel empowered to move forward in your healing journey in a way that makes sense to you.

We compare the healing journey to a seed that sprouts in different directions. You might plant a seed of healing by working on your self-worth through practicing positive self-talk and self-compassion. As the sprout of self-worth grows, it can branch out into other areas, such as increasing your confidence in friendships, relationships at work, and even how you manage your finances. Focusing on any aspect of healing and recovery from abuse can enhance your confidence and self-worth, which, in turn, can positively impact your financial well-being. Similarly, if you start by addressing your financial goals and achieving greater economic well-being, you'll likely find that your efforts in this area also support your overall healing.

Connecting with the Right Sources of Support

For many survivors, seeking the support of trained professionals can be a key resource. This might include therapy with a mental health professional who is experienced in working with survivors of abuse or seeking therapy to focus on navigating your mindset and experiences with money. Additionally, you may benefit from working with credible consumer credit counseling or financial education services. As we shared throughout this book, you can visit our book website (www.sourceforsurvivors.info/financialabuse) to find resources that may be useful for you.

Whether you work with professionals in your local community or seek virtual services from someone outside your immediate area, it's important to seek credible resources. Don't hesitate to ask questions of any professional with whom you're considering working to ensure they have your best interests at heart, can work with you in a supportive and non-judgmental manner, and are knowledgeable in their field.

We also highlight the importance of connecting with informal sources of social support, such as building meaningful friendships, attending survivor support groups, and getting involved with positive, encouraging groups and organizations in your community. These might include groups centered around shared religious or spiritual beliefs, financial goals, or fun and uplifting interests, like hobbies or physical activities.

Having a support system, whether from professionals or a kind group of friends can go a long way toward helping you feel supported and connected. This is especially important for survivors, given the isolation that often accompanies abusive relationships. Remember that you also have value to bring to your relationships and friendships with others. If self-doubt is holding you back and you lack the confidence to seek out new connections, this may be an area to explore with a trained mental health professional. Give yourself time to learn to embrace support from the kind, caring people in your life. Trust your instincts and set healthy boundaries to limit the effects of any toxic or unhealthy relationships you encounter. Especially after experiencing the harmful effects of an abusive relationship, it can be incredibly empowering for survivors to nurture safe, healthy, supportive relationships in all areas of life.

Staying Focused When You Feel Overwhelmed

It can feel overwhelming to process all the layers of impacts that abuse may have had on your life. This is a natural feeling, and we've experienced it in our own lives as survivors. We encourage you to focus on taking one step at a time, however big or small, and to trust your intuition about the area(s) of focus that will be most meaningful and useful for you at any given time. If it's helpful to you, think of the journey of recovering from an abusive relationship not as a destination or finish line you must reach, but as an ongoing process where you can celebrate and reflect on your progress along the way.

Sometimes, the first steps in the healing journey can be the most daunting and complicated. It takes time to build momentum and feel a sense of progress. Focus on the steps you can take right now, and give yourself plenty of grace and patience throughout the process. Sometimes, progress might seem small—like saving just $5 in one month like the example we shared in Chapter 8. Avoid the temptation to jump to the conclusion that you'll only be able to save $5 a month for the rest of your life! Celebrating even seemingly small successes is important because they can help you build confidence and set the stage for further growth and action later on. Maybe you're saving $5 a month for a few months, and then eventually you can start to increase your savings rate gradually over time.

We also acknowledge that setbacks can be part of the process. Sticking with our example, you might save $5 for several months and feel good about your progress, but an unexpected expense sets you back $200 the following month. Ugh! It's natural to feel frustration and disappointment when setbacks arise, but remember that setbacks are temporary and a natural part of striving to make positive life changes. Even significant setbacks don't have to derail you completely; often, they can help you learn where you may need to tweak or adjust your plans.

Have supporters around you who can cheer you on and provide encouragement—even in the face of setbacks. These supporters may also offer practical and tangible help when needed and help you problem-solve and get back on track when setbacks arise.

Strengthening Your Relationship with Yourself

Additionally, we encourage you to build a healthier, more supportive relationship with *yourself* throughout the healing process. Pay close attention to how you talk to yourself and treat yourself as you move forward, including when setbacks occur. If you notice harsh, negative self-talk, try to shift to a more compassionate, kind, and self-supportive tone, as if speaking gently to a child or a friend.

Sometimes, we need external validation and support along the healing journey, but flexing our self-validation muscles is also empowering. There will be moments when we need to remind and encourage ourselves of just how amazing we really are! Self-validation can be nurtured through journaling, where you reflect on your progress and affirm your strengths. Other practical approaches, like placing encouraging notes on your bathroom mirror or refrigerator, can serve as daily reminders of the positive messages you want to focus on throughout your healing journey.

In the area of your finances, we invite you to intentionally develop your sense of self-efficacy around your capacity to set and achieve financial goals. The Cambridge Dictionary (n.d.) defines self-efficacy as "a person's belief that they can be successful when carrying out a particular task." Self-efficacy regarding your finances goes beyond a general sense of self-confidence or self-worth, and it focuses on your belief in your knowledge, skills, and competence for managing your finances and achieving your financial goals.

Building self-efficacy takes time, especially when an abuser has systematically diminished your confidence. Self-efficacy around financial matters also can be difficult if you did not receive much financial literacy education growing up, as well as if you observed or experienced poor money management in your family-of-origin or your own past experiences. However, as you continue to move forward in your healing journey, implementing the strategies you've learned and working toward your financial goals and dreams, remember: *you can do this.*

You have the capacity within you to set financial goals and see those goals through to completion. Sometimes, you may abandon goals that you outgrow and replace them with new goals that feel right to you at that time. Know this is part of the process. When you're working toward financial goals, you might need support along the way. Seeking help doesn't mean there's something wrong with you or that you can't achieve your goals; in fact, many significant goals and dreams are reached only with the support of trained professionals and other supporters. Consider how even professional athletes rely heavily on coaches, trainers, and teammates throughout their careers. Finding and using the right kinds of help and support are essential to the growth process and can bolster your confidence and belief in your ability to heal and move toward greater financial well-being.

Final Reminders: Empowerment and Freedom along the Healing Journey

As much as possible, strive to empower yourself throughout your healing journey. We understand this may not be easy—feeling disempowered is a common experience for many survivors who have been in abusive relationships due to the effects of the abuser's actions. However, reclaiming your sense of empowerment is possible and important as you move forward.

Your abuser likely tried to restrict your freedom and autonomy throughout your relationship. As you move forward toward healing, it may feel pretty uncomfortable at first to have so much more freedom than you're used to. Allow yourself the time you need to get to know yourself again, search deeply within yourself for your heart's hopes and dreams, and plan to take the right next steps for you in your journey. Avoid rushing into decisions you're not ready to make yet. Healing takes time.

The journey toward healing and recovering from an abusive relationship can take time. How much time varies from person to person. For some survivors, there is a specific endpoint at which they feel they are fully "healed." For others, however, the healing journey is an ongoing process that may last a lifetime. (Both of us tend to believe our journeys are lifelong ones, and we embrace the hope that we will have opportunities to continue to grow, learn, and heal throughout the rest of our lives.)

In Chapter 1, we outlined three big-picture takeaway messages that we hoped readers would gain by reading this book. Let's revisit these here as we conclude the book.

First, we've focused on the significant potential financial consequences of abusive relationships, while also acknowledging that survivors often lack access to the support and information needed to overcome economic challenges and move toward financial well-being. Throughout this book, we aimed to bridge this gap by offering insights and practical strategies to help survivors rebuild (or perhaps build for the first time) their financial well-being. Every step a survivor takes toward economic stability strengthens their own life and contributes to the well-being of their families and communities. We hope that the knowledge and tools provided in this book empower readers to build a solid financial foundation, ultimately creating a ripple effect of economic resilience and empowerment in your own life and the lives of your loved ones.

Second, we've aimed to normalize that personal finances can be intimidating, while also offering encouragement and tools to increase your financial literacy and develop a vision for what financial well-being looks like for you. We understand that managing finances can feel overwhelming, especially if you feel like you're starting from scratch. However, by gradually building your financial knowledge, you can begin to reduce any fears and anxieties that accompany this topic for you. Whether you're just starting to learn the basics or already have financial expertise, there's always room to grow. As you work toward overcoming the financial repercussions of abuse, you can enhance your sense of financial well-being and security. No matter where you start, your finances ultimately can become a source of confidence and empowerment as you set goals, work toward them, and increase your financial freedom.

And finally, we hope you've joined us in noticing the potential opportunities for healing that can come as you take action and make progress toward increasing your financial well-being. Focusing on your financial well-being isn't just about numbers and bank account balances—it's about creating pathways for personal growth and recovery. Tracking your progress toward financial goals can provide tangible signs of improvement, and even seemingly minor steps can lead to forward momentum. As you expand your financial knowledge, skills, and resources, you can also open up more choices and opportunities in other aspects of your life. These choices may bring a greater sense of freedom and empowerment, which is invaluable for survivors of abuse. The journey toward financial well-being is not just about economic security; it's about reclaiming your power and autonomy in ways that enrich your entire life.

We celebrate the courageous journey you've undertaken by exploring the ideas in this book. We hope you've gained practical tools and insights to apply to your life, and we encourage you to continue taking one step at a time. Healing is not a linear process, and the path forward will include a mix of ups, downs, challenges, setbacks, and triumphs. But every step you take is valuable and a testament to your resilience and strength.

Take the time you need to process the information and insights from this book. Consider rereading sections as needed. Feel free to return to the earlier chapters' reflection exercises to remind yourself of your goals, progress, and intentions. And remember, you are moving toward creating a bright, secure future filled with the peace and stability you deserve.

We are both deeply proud of the progress you've made and will continue to make in your journey toward healing and financial empowerment. Thank you for trusting us to be part of your journey. May you continue to grow, heal richer, and thrive as you move forward in your life.

Reference List

Chapter 1

Allstate Foundation (n.d.). Relationship abuse: Disrupt the cycle of relationship abuse. https://www.allstatecorporation.com/the-allstate-foundation/relationship-abuse.aspx

Bechard, C. W. (2022). Forgive yourself and overcome money shame. *University of Illinois College of Agricultural, Consumer, & Environmental Sciences: Illinois Extension Blog.* https://extension.illinois.edu/blogs/fearless-financial-future/2022-02-08-forgive-yourself-and-overcome-money-shame

Consumer Financial Protection Bureau (n.d.). Financial well-being resources. https://www.consumerfinance.gov/consumer-tools/educator-tools/financial-well-being-resources

Gladstone, J. J., Jachimowicz, J. M., Greenberg, A. E., & Galinsky, A. D. (2021). Financial shame spirals: How shame intensifies financial hardship. *Organizational Behavior and Human Decision Processes, 167,* 42-56. https://doi.org/10.1016/j.obhdp.2021.06.002.

Next Gen Personal Finance (n.d.). Live U.S. Dashboard: Guarantee States. https://www.ngpf.org/live-us-dashboard/

Gladstone, J. J., Jachimowicz, J. M., Greenberg, A. E., & Galinsky, A. D. (2021). Financial shame spirals: How shame intensifies financial hardship. *Organizational Behavior and Human Decision Processes, 167,* 42-56. https://doi.org/10.1016/j.obhdp.2021.06.002.

Chapter 2

Craig, H., & Kippert, A. (2022). What is the cycle of abuse? Domesticshelters.org. https://www.domesticshelters.org/articles/identifying-abuse/what-is-the-cycle-of-abuse

Holtzworth-Munroe, A., & Stuart, G. L. (1994). Typologies of male batterers: Three subtypes and the differences among them. *Psychological Bulletin, 116*(3), 476-97. doi: 10.1037/0033-2909.116.3.476.

Jacobson, N., & Gottman, J. (2007). *When men batter women.* Simon & Schuster.

King, K., Murray, C. E., Crowe, A., Hunnicutt, G., Lundgren, K., & Olson, L. (2017). The Costs of Recovery: Intimate Partner Violence Survivors' Experiences of Financial Recovery From Abuse. *The Family Journal, 25*(3), 230-238.https://doi.org/10.1177/1066480717710656

Murray, C. E., and Graves, K. N. (2012). *Responding to family violence: A research-based guide for mental health professionals.* New York: Routledge.

National Domestic Violence Hotline (n.d.). *Types of abuse.* https://www.thehotline.org/resources/types-of-abuse/

Chapter 3

Weitzman, S. (2001). *Not to people like us: Hidden abuse in upscale marriages.* Basic Books.

Chapter 4

Murray, C. E. (2023). Introduction to the Pathway for Survivors: 6 Commitments for Triumphing Over Abuse. *The Source for Survivors Blog,* November 22, 2023. https://www.sourceforsurvivors.info/

survivorsblog/introduction-to-the-pathway-for-survivors-6-commitments-for-triumphing-over-abuse

Murray, C. E. (2024). The Pathways for Supporting Survivors Model: 6 Commitments for Survivors of Abuse and Community Support Resources. *The Source for Survivors.* https://www.sourceforsurvivors.info/about.html

Neff, K. (n.d.). *Publications by Kristin Neff and Colleagues.* https://self-compassion.org/the-research/

Chapter 5

Brown, B. (2013). *Shame vs. guilt.* https://brenebrown.com/articles/2013/01/15/shame-v-guilt/

Murray, C. E., & Crowe, A. (2016). *Overcoming the Stigma around Intimate Partner Violence.* New York: Routledge Mental Health.

Neff, K. (n.d.). *What is self-compassion?* https://self-compassion.org/what-is-self-compassion/#what-is-self-compassion

Chapter 6

Consumer Financial Protection Bureau (n.d.). Financial well-being resources. https://www.consumerfinance.gov/consumer-tools/educator-tools/financial-well-being-resources

National Financial Educators Council (2023). *Financial illiteracy cost Americans $1,506 in 2023.* https://www.financialeducatorscouncil.org/financial-illiteracy-costs/

National Financial Educators Council (n.d.) *Cost of financial illiteracy.* https://www.financialeducatorscouncil.org/wp-content/uploads/Cost-of-financial-illiteracy.pdf

Neff, K. (n.d.). *What is self-compassion?* https://self-compassion.org/what-is-self-compassion/#what-is-self-compassion

Chapter 7

Burnett, B., & Evans, D. (2016). *Designing your life: How to build a well-lived, joyful life.* Knopf.

Cameron, J. (2016). *The Artist's Way: 30th anniversary edition.* TarcherPerigee.

Chapter 8

Investopedia (2024). *Debt avalanche: Meaning, pros and cons, and examples.* https://www.investopedia.com/terms/d/debt-avalanche.asp

Ramsey Solutions (2024). *How to get out of debt with the debt snowball plan.* https://www.ramseysolutions.com/debt/get-out-of-debt-with-the-debt-snowball-plan

Ramsey Solutions (n.d.). *The 7 Baby Steps.* https://www.ramseysolutions.com/dave-ramsey-7-baby-steps

Chapter 9

Bolles, R. N. (2022, Revised edition). *What color is your parachute? Your guide to a lifetime of meaningful work and career success.* Ten Speed Press.

Chapter 10

Cambridge Dictionary (n.d.). *Definition of self-efficacy.* https://dictionary.cambridge.org/us/dictionary/english/self-efficacy

Author Biographies

Christine E. Murray, Ph.D., is a Professor of Counseling at the Townsend Institute at Concordia University Irvine, as well as the Founder of Start Here Counseling & Consulting, PLLC. She is also a Professor Emerita at The University of North Carolina at Greensboro (UNCG). She retired from UNCG during the summer of 2024 after 19 years of service as a faculty member in the Department of Counseling and Educational Development. From 2019 to 2023, she also served as the Director of the UNCG Center for Youth, Family, and Community Partnerships.

Christine earned her Ph.D. and M.Ed./Ed.S. in Marriage and Family Counseling and Counselor Education from the University of Florida, as well as her B.A. in Psychology and Sociology from Duke University.

Christine has over two decades of experience working in the mental health field. Based in Greensboro, North Carolina, she is a Licensed Marriage and Family Therapist (LMFT) and Licensed Clinical Mental Health Counselor (LCMHC) in North Carolina, as well as a Licensed Marriage and Family Therapist (LMFT) and Licensed Professional Counselor (LPC) in her home state of Pennsylvania.

Throughout her career, much of Christine's work has focused on supporting survivors of domestic violence in the long-term recovery process and strengthening community response systems to better support victims and survivors as they move toward safety and healing.

Christine brings her own lived experience as a survivor of past abuse to her work, including as Founder of The Source for Survivors resource and as author of six previous books that include the following: *Triumph Over Abuse: Healing, Recovery, and Purpose after an Abusive Relationship* and *The Verbal Abuse Recovery Workbook: Healing from*

Emotional Abuse. To learn more about Christine's work, please visit https://www.christinemurray.info/.

Eileen Martin, MSW, LCSW, is a Licensed Clinical Social Worker and Founder of the Center for Counseling and Healing. With a focus on supporting survivors of abuse through her therapy practice, Eileen is trained as a family trauma professional and has extensive expertise in interpersonal violence, domestic violence advocacy, and crisis intervention. She has contributed her professional knowledge through multiple podcast platforms and in *Self* magazine, and she has volunteered as an advocate and speaker for the Family Justice Center VOICES committee.

Currently, Eileen is developing domestic violence training programs for therapists to deepen their understanding and ability to support survivors. As an abuse survivor herself, she is dedicated to ending intimate partner violence by creating safe spaces where survivors can re-author their lives. In her free time, Eileen enjoys photography as a mindfulness practice and exploring National Parks with her husband. You can visit https://www.centerforcounselingandhealing.org/ for more information.